Contents

NEBS MANAGEMENT DEVELOPMENT

SUPER SERIES

THIRD EDITION

Managing Information

Communicating in Groups

Published for

NEBS Management   *by*

Pergamon
Flexible
Learning

Pergamon Flexible Learning
An imprint of Butterworth-Heinemann
Linacre House, Jordan Hill, Oxford OX2 8DP
225 Wildwood Avenue, Woburn, MA 01801-2041
A division of Reed Educational and Professional Publishing Ltd

A member of the Reed Elsevier plc group

OXFORD   AUCKLAND   BOSTON
JOHANNESBURG   MELBOURNE   NEW DELHI

First published 1986
Second edition 1991
Third edition 1997
Reprinted 1998, 1999, 2000

© NEBS Management 1986, 1991, 1997

British Library Cataloguing in Publication Data
A catalogue record for this book is available from the British Library

ISBN 0 7506 3330 1

The author acknowledges the following publisher for their
kind permission to allow reproduction of copyright material:
Oxford University Press (Shorter Oxford English Dictionary).

The views expressed in this work are those
of the authors and do not necessarily reflect
those of the National Examining Board for
Supervision and Management or of the publisher.

NEBS Management Project Manager: Diana Thomas
Author: Howard Senter
Editor: Ian Bloor
Series Editor: Diana Thomas
Based on previous material by: Joe Johnson
Composition by Genesis Typesetting, Rochester, Kent
Printed and bound in Great Britain by MPG Books Ltd, Bodmin, Cornwall

Workbook introduction

1 NEBS Management Super Series 3 study links

Here are the workbook titles in each module which link with *Communicating in Groups*, should you wish to extend your study to other Super Series workbooks. There is a brief description of each workbook in the User Guide.

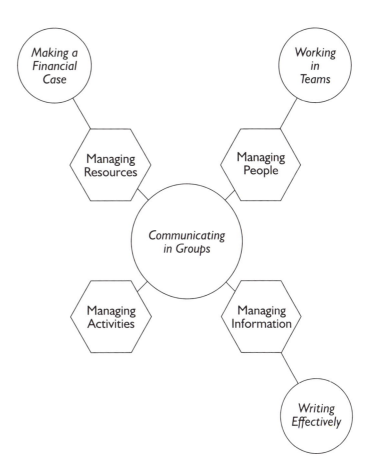

2 S/NVQ links

This workbook relates to the following elements:

C1.1   Develop your own skills to improve your performance
C1.2   Manage your time to meet your objectives
C4.2   Gain the trust and support of your manager
C12.1   Plan the work of teams and individuals
D1.1   Gather required information
D1.2   Inform and advise others

It is designed to help you to demonstrate the following Personal Competences:

■ communicating;
■ influencing others.

3 Workbook objectives

Communication is central to human life, society and work, and everyone does a great deal of communicating – even people who don't think they're very good at it.

Communication has several functions. At one level, there is entertainment, where our role is largely passive. We read, listen to the radio, watch the TV. At a more important level, there is communication as 'social glue'. Just like chimps, whales and starlings, the constant communicating that goes on in our social groups helps to stabilize and cement them.

When someone says 'we don't communicate any more', it is shorthand for saying a family or social relationship has broken down.

People shouldn't neglect this relationship-building aspect of communication when at work. It is fundamental to successful management, teamwork and good working relationships all round. **Simply by communicating** a manager, supervisor or team leader is achieving something useful.

However, this aspect of communication is largely incidental. Work is about using resources in order to achieve objectives, and communication plays a central role in this. Managers, supervisors and team leaders need to brief, instruct, inform and advise people at various levels in order to do their jobs properly. They also need to listen, observe and record.

We all have the basic ability to do this, but if we can do it better, then we will achieve more impressive results, and sooner or later the rewards will flow. 'Doing it better' is about developing more advanced skills in communication, particularly at the more formal level, where the audiences may be larger.

In this workbook we will consider how to frame messages that work better, and how to choose the most appropriate channels of communication. We will go further – to think about how to influence people, rather than simply instructing or informing them.

In general, we will be focusing on how to communicate effectively in the more formal and complex situations, especially those where groups of people are involved. This will take us into the field of team briefings, formal meetings, negotiations, presentations and speeches to audiences of total strangers. These present more of a challenge simply because they are more formal and because the audiences are larger.

However, though the situations are different the principles are much the same as for any kind of communication. And communicating in groups is something that everyone can learn to do better.

3.1 Objectives

When you have completed this workbook you will be better able to:

- frame effective messages and choose the most appropriate channels through which to send them;
- plan and chair meetings;
- prepare and make an effective contribution to a meeting;
- plan, prepare and deliver an effective speech or presentation.

4 Activity planner

The following Activities require some planning so you may want to look at these now.

- Activity 12, in which you are asked to prepare and rehearse a team briefing.

- Activity 18, which asks you to observe and comment on a typical management meeting.

- Activity 28, which is also about meetings, only this time you are thinking about how the meeting is prepared and managed.

- Activity 37, in which you are asked to prepare a short presentation about the work of your team.

- Activity 48, about recognizing and controlling your own physical and verbal mannerisms as a speaker.

Workbook introduction

Portfolio of evidence

Some or all of these Activities may provide the basis of evidence for your S/NVQ portfolio. All Portfolio Activities and the Work-based assignment are signposted with this icon.

The icon states the elements to which the Portfolio Activities and Work-based assignment relate.

Session A Communicating at work

1 Introduction

Humans communicate a great deal. In fact, communication is what makes us – and our world – what we are. Without it, civilization would be impossible and there would be no organizations of any description.

Communication is therefore both basic and essential in every aspect of our lives.

We communicate for a purpose. We use communication:

- to co-ordinate our actions;
- to explain new things to one another;
- to organize our social relationships;
- to entertain one another.

Probably the last of these – entertainment – is the role that most communication plays. It would include:

- most TV watching and radio listening;
- most reading;
- most personal conversations.

We won't be dealing with the passive aspects of communication – watching, listening, reading – in this workbook. However, we will need to think about conversations, because the way we talk to one another plays an important role in creating and regulating our social relationships.

Even the most casual and 'off-the-record' chat can help:

- mould attitudes;
- strengthen – or damage – the bonds between us;
- show us where we stand in relation to one another.

The meaning of this for managers, supervisors and team leaders should be obvious. When you speak to colleagues or your team:

- you **often** do so in order to achieve a particular objective;
- but you **always** affect the way they relate to you.

If you communicate well, you can strengthen bonds, create loyalty, build morale and improve productivity. If you communicate poorly, or not enough, the opposite can happen.

I

2 How communication works

At work, when managers, supervisors and team leaders communicate, they frequently do so in order to achieve specific objectives. This **purposive** communication is intended to result in changes of a desirable kind, such as:

- an action being performed;
- an error being corrected;
- the receiver knowing or understanding something new.

2.1 Purposes and effects

Every act of communication also has an incidental effect on the way the people involved relate to one another. Since these are **working relationships**, this incidental aspect of communication is also important.

Activity 1

2 mins

- Raj announced to the team that there would be a fire drill at 10.00 am the following Thursday.

What purpose does this communication serve?

What effects is it likely to have on working relationships.

There are two purposes behind this simple communication: we can call them the **open** agenda and the **hidden** agenda.

The open agenda is about **practical objectives** – in this case to inform the team about the fire drill so that they will be prepared for it.

Information is empowering.

The hidden agenda is about **feelings and attitudes**: keeping the team informed encourages trust and team spirit. It also helps the individual team members feel more involved with events, and hence more empowered.

If Raj's communication hits its target, the world is changed in three small but useful ways:

- the team members possess some information they did not have before;
- they may take action – for example to avoid starting any long or complicated task just before the fire drill is due;
- their confidence in the team leader is strengthened.

2.2 Feedback

Imagine that Raj sits in an enclosed office and cannot see or hear the other team members; they cannot see or hear him. When he wishes to speak to the team, he uses a microphone connected to a loudspeaker outside his office.

There is no doubt that everyone can hear him. The question is: how does Raj know whether anything happens as a result?

Activity 2

Now let's imagine that the walls of Raj's office suddenly vanish, and he makes the same communication in an ordinary human way.

Now how does he know whether anything happens as a result?

The answer is something that we all experience every day:

- as Raj starts to speak, the team members first show that they are **reacting** by paying attention, usually by pausing in their work and turning to look at him;
- second, they show signs of **understanding** his message, by nodding, making notes or other visual signals;
- third, they may demonstrate **attention** by seeking clarification – by asking questions;
- fourth, they may signal **acceptance** of the message by nodding, or saying 'OK' etc.

Depending on what the communication was about, its outcome may be fed back to Raj by the team members:

■ verbally confirming;
■ or demonstrating in some way;
  that they have complied with the message.

Clearly, communication is a **two-way process.** Messages or information pass from one person to another, but messages also come back to the sender.

We can show the process in a diagram like this:

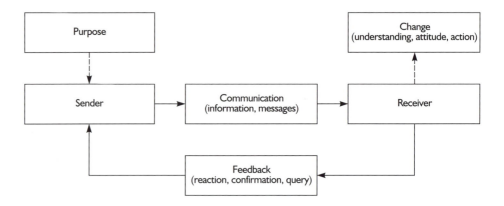

Where several people are involved – in a team meeting, for example – the picture obviously becomes much more complicated. Any individual may be a sender at one moment and a receiver the next; and there may be several sets of communications overlapping and mingling together. This is why one of the rules for formal meetings is that only one person at a time may speak.

Whatever the situation, if you want your communication to succeed, it pays to concentrate on:

■ framing clear and credible messages;
■ checking that they have arrived and have been understood.

Clarity and checking are particularly important in negotiations, where two or more people exchange a whole series of fairly detailed messages and small changes in meaning may be extremely significant.

3 The message

Now let's look at what is actually said or written.

3.1 Spoken messages

■ 'Er, are you busy right now? I mean, is what you're doing really urgent … of course it is, I know it's all important … only these orders ought to go out tonight if possible … could you try and fit them in? Perhaps when you've finished the others? OK then I'll leave it with you …'

Activity 3

The words in the above case study were spoken by a team leader.

What do you think the outcome will be?

_____

Comment briefly on the effectiveness of this communication.

_____
_____
_____

There may have been some feedback confirming that the orders will be sent out tonight. The other person may have smiled and nodded, or given the thumbs up. But on the face of it, we don't know – and neither does the speaker.

This is a very poor piece of communication:

■ the speaker obviously wants the orders to 'go out tonight', but fails to give a clear instruction to that effect;
■ he or she clearly lacks assertiveness;
■ he or she seems lacking in authority.

In practice, this is a recipe for trouble. The speaker may **believe** that he or she has made it clear that the orders are urgent; the other person's understanding, however, is that it is up to him or her to decide. Tomorrow, when it turns out the orders didn't go, there may be a row.

Activity 4

4 mins

Which of the following would be good rules for making sure your message gets across?

1	Repeat the central message at least once.	☐
2	State clearly what you want done, when and by whom.	☐
3	Speak loudly and clearly.	☐
4	Keep it short and simple.	☐
5	Be assertive, even aggressive.	☐
6	Use words and phrases that you are confident the receiver(s) will understand.	☐
7	Check that they understand.	☐
8	Use visual means in preference to verbal ones.	☐

Numbers 1, 2, 4, 6 and 7 are all excellent rules for effective communication. The others need some comment.

3   Speak loudly and clearly

It is always better to speak clearly. Speaking loudly **may** be useful in a noisy environment, or when the audience is spread over a large area. However, in ordinary situations it may make you sound like a school teacher addressing a class of six-year-olds.

5   Be assertive, even aggressive

Assertiveness is usually good: it means making it clear what you want, without beating about the bush and without being aggressive. Aggressiveness always provokes a bad reaction and damages relations between people.

8   Use visual means in preference to verbal ones – pictures in preference to words and numbers

I hear and I forget.
I see and I remember.
I do and I understand.

This can be good advice, but it depends on the situation. It is much easier to explain production output trends with a graph (visual) than with a table (verbal), and easier with a table than with words, whether written or spoken. However, the best plan is usually to **mix** visual and verbal means: research has repeatedly proved that we remember images better than words.

You might like to add three further rules for verbal communication to the list above:

- Speak calmly and at a gentle pace.
- Limit the amount of information you try to communicate.
- Make sure your body language matches your message.

We will come back to body language later (in Section 6 of this session).

3.2 Written messages

Most of the rules for spoken communication apply equally to written messages. However, you may have noticed that we tend to be much more formal when we're writing. In speech we are usually quite *in*formal.

To see the difference, you only need to write down word for word what someone says. It will usually look very messy in print.

The advantage of writing, however, is that we usually have longer to absorb it. Spoken words are gone almost instantly.

Activity 5

2 mins

This suggests some simple rules about when it is better to communicate in writing. What would you say they were?

_____

_____

In general, it is preferable to communicate in writing when we want to:

- send several messages, rather than just one or two;
- send longer and more complicated messages;
- include more background detail and supporting documentation.

3.3 Using your authority

Messages get through better, and arguments carry more weight, when they are delivered with authority.

This means two things:

- the messages and arguments themselves must be credible and coherent;
- the person delivering them must inspire respect and confidence.

Authority influences people, but what exactly is it?

At one level authority derives from your title, your **formal** position in the organization. Most managers, supervisors and team leaders will find a paragraph in their Job Description headed something like 'extent of authority'. This explains what people and other resources they are **authorized** to make decisions about. The people concerned are expected to comply.

However, managing with authority isn't just about saying 'I'm the boss here and you'd better do what I say'.

The people who work in your organization are all working of their own free will. They may want their job, but they may not want it badly enough to put up with a dictatorial management. In practice, authority mainly depends on a person being able to demonstrate:

EXTENSION I
NEBS Management
Workbook
Managing with Authority.

■ expertise;
■ competence;
■ fairness;
■ consistency in making and implementing decisions.

So managers, supervisors and team leaders have a degree of formal authority, but this isn't enough to ensure that when you communicate, you achieve your objectives. You also need:

■ to prepare;
■ to understand your audience;
■ to phrase your messages clearly;
■ to be assertive;
■ to match your body language to your messages.

And it always pays to keep your messages short and simple.

4 The channel

So far we have described a limited number of channels of communication – the kinds of media used to transmit our messages. However, there are quite a lot of different channels available today, especially in view of advances in digital electronic information technology.

Activity 6

5 mins

Think of all the different channels you might use to communicate with colleagues or team members, and write them in the blank spaces below.

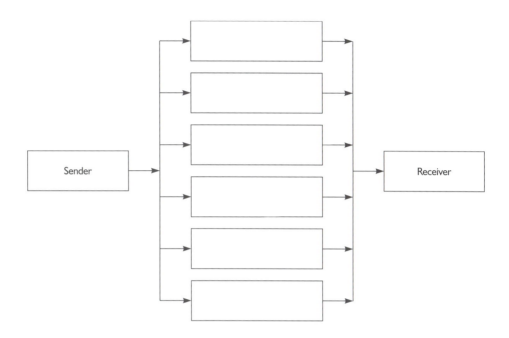

See page 88 for my suggestions.

You may have thought of other channels, depending on the kind of work you do, and technology is steadily providing new options. Videophones are now available in a limited way, and videoconferencing – where two or more sites are linked by satellite transmission – is considered a possible competitor to business class airline travel!

Conferencing by telephone (voice-only) is already well-established, and keyboard-based forums via the Internet are becoming increasingly popular.

It only needs a few moments' thought about this list to show that the choice of channels of communication depends on the situation being addressed.

For example, if the team is upset by rumours about possible redundancies, sending them a memo is not the ideal channel to choose.

Activity 7

6 mins

What channel – or channels – would you choose in the following situations?

1   A team based 100 miles away needs your technical advice on a complex matter.

Channel(s) of choice: _____

2   The Personnel Manager wants a report on an incident that occurred a few days ago.

Channel(s) of choice: _____

3   You need to announce details of a competition open to staff members and their families.

Channel(s) of choice: _____

4   Your telephone and fax extension numbers have changed, and all colleagues need to be informed.

Channel(s) of choice: _____

5   There are rumours of redundancies. The team want to know what you have heard

Channel(s) of choice: _____

When you need to communicate with people who are a long way away (1), speaking on the **telephone** or sending a **letter** may be enough. If the matter is urgent, your letter can be **faxed** or **e-mailed**. However, if the issue is complicated, you may need to be there **in person** to explain, demonstrate and answer questions. An interactive video link, if this technology is available, might also be an option.

A formal report (2) needs to be put in **writing**, though both you and the Personnel Manager might well want to discuss the matter person to person. A written report can go **on the record**, and this may be important.

A competition (3) is generally not urgent, and does not require you to put your personal credibility behind any statement. However, there may be fairly complicated details that ought to be made available. Thus while you might want to **speak about** the competition to team members, the ideal channel would be a notice pinned up where everyone could see it, or an article in the staff newsletter.

Where there's more than one channel that you might use, choose the simplest and cheapest.

In situation 4, you could phone everyone up and tell them, or send round a memo to everyone. However, since you are giving the same information to everyone, the simplest and cheapest options would be (a) to **e-mail** details to everyone inside the organization, and (b) to send a standard letter to all your outside contacts.

Situation 5 obviously makes demands on your leadership and personal credibility. It would be a mistake to use any 'distance' method of responding. You should be prepared to talk with the team in person, even if your message consists of admitting that you don't know the answer and promising to find out.

We can establish some guidelines about choosing channels for communications at work:

■ face-to-face communication – because of the amount of human contact involved – is the best choice where good working relationships are at stake;

■ written communication – alone or as a back-up – is appropriate where something needs to:

- ■ contain a lot of detail;
- ■ be considered at length;
- ■ go on the record;

■ new digital communications technology provides extra options for when speed and distance are factors, and when people at several different locations need to be contacted.

5 Groups and teams

Communicating with groups is different from communicating with individuals:

■ the fact that there is an **audience** may put more pressure on the speaker – especially if he or she is inclined to be nervous or self-conscious;

■ it is a more complex task – there are more people to take account of;

■ groups behave differently from the individuals who compose them – groups may take on a personality of their own.

There are some important distinctions between a **group** and a **team**.

5.1 Defining the difference

The following example sums up the difference between a 'group' and a 'team'.

Activity 8

4 mins

■ 'As the busker began to play, a handful of passers-by stopped to listen.'

We can think of these listeners as a group, but all that they had in common was the fact that they happened to be passing by when the busker began to play. Apart from this, they may well have been complete strangers.

How does a group differ from a team?

There is a strong clue in the way we asked the question. The members of a group may have little in common. The members of a team, by contrast, have – or should have – a lot in common.

The people who form a work team are expected:

■ to **know each other**:

- they will understand each others' abilities and interests, strengths and weaknesses, and will be comfortable in each others' company;
- they may well have social contact outside work;

■ to **share values and goals**:

- they will work together to achieve common objectives;
- they will tend to have similar attitudes to the organization, the job, the team leader and people outside the team;

■ to **possess a sense of common identity and team spirit**:

- they will support one another;
- they will help to train and develop one another;
- they will work flexibly, exchanging roles and tasks when appropriate.

Some teams are more developed than others, but a team is clearly a very different organism from a group.

5.2 Random groups

■ This story was told to me by an old man who was brought up in Poland during the 1920s. It tells us something interesting about group dynamics.
'When I was a small child – seven or eight – I was often sent to get the cows in for milking. I used to ask myself – How come a small boy with a stick can make these 20 big cows do what he wants? Later I realized. Each cow looked around and thought – I'm up against 19 cows and a small boy. I'd better play safe!'

This doesn't mean that people in groups necessarily behave in a sheep-like way. Human beings are conscious and have will-power; they can discuss, argue and object. However, it is generally accepted that membership of a group does affect the behaviour of individuals:

■ individuals in groups may feel isolated and lack confidence;
■ they may feel it is 'safer' to go with the majority;
■ this can tend to reinforce the confidence of the majority;
■ which can in turn give the individuals confidence to do and say things they would not otherwise do and say.

This means that:

■ a single strong personality can sometimes influence a group in a particular direction;
■ an organized minority within a group of people who don't know each other can often determine the group's attitude and actions;
■ the attitudes and intentions of such random groups can be quite unstable, and can swing first one way and then the other.

Activity 9

Which of these statements points to the best strategy for a person wishing to influence a group?

1   Take a firm line, try to dominate, and if necessary intimidate the group.

2   Start by convincing one or two members of the group and use them to influence the rest.

3   Watch carefully for reactions and modify your approach in the light of these.

The third statement is the most useful. It is highly unwise to try to intimidate a group – or a team for that matter. They can easily react against you. Nor is it necessarily easy to sway a group from the outside.

One obvious factor about a more or less random group is that they are strangers: an outsider doesn't know them any more than they know each other. For this reason, the second statement is also the wrong choice – you don't know enough about the members of a group to identify the 'opinion-formers'. This approach can however work with a team, as we shall see.

Only by paying very careful attention to reactions can a speaker tell what they feel and which way they are capable of moving. However, it takes a great deal of skill and experience to communicate effectively with random groups.

In practice, few of the groups that managers, supervisors and team leaders encounter at work are likely to be truly random. In most cases they will work for your own, or a similar, organization. They will share at least some attitudes, values and knowledge.

Also, most people are used to a culture of attending meetings and listening to speakers. Even audiences you don't know will generally listen patiently, if not with any great enthusiasm.

5.3 Teams have values

■ Simone was sent over to the warehouse to talk to the pickers about new rules for disposing of waste packing materials. The pickers, who were a notoriously difficult bunch, shuffled and sniggered through Simone's five-minute presentation. There were several interruptions to ask deliberately silly questions. Simone's confidence was badly dented. She finished by saying, 'You may think it's a joke, but you'll be laughing on the other side of your faces when Mr Khan does his next inspection.' This was greeted with derision.

Activity 10

What was the problem in the case study you have just read? What could Simone have done about it?

_____

_____

The pickers were a team, with common values and attitudes. The problem was that their values were negative ones, from Simone's point of view. The pickers' culture allowed them to break all the normal rules of politeness in order to make her life difficult. Simone's own outburst at the end will only have made things worse. The episode will have damaged her authority, and her attempt to get an important message through will probably have failed.

A team, then, starts out with a strong sense of its identity, position and values, and is capable of maintaining them in the face of outside pressure.

When you are addressing your own team, you should be able to assume that they will have a positive attitude toward you. When you are communicating with them there should be no major barriers to overcome.

Teams are likely to resist challenges to their accepted beliefs, attitudes and practices.

With an uncommitted or actually hostile team, it is different. Even the world's greatest orator would have trouble winning them over in five minutes flat. You need to do some work behind the scenes in order to overcome – or at least weaken – some of the barriers.

Activity 11

4 mins

Here are two approaches that Simone might adopt towards a team with a strongly negative position. Comment briefly on them.

1 'Come on, guys, give me a break. I've had a hard day and I could do without all this aggro.'

2 'I've come to explain this new procedure to you because Mr Khan has instructed me to. So let's just get it over with, shall we?'

In the first version, Simone is basically pleading with the pickers to be nice to her. In the second she is invoking Mr Khan's authority – passing the buck, in other words. Both are poor approaches, because they undermine Simone's authority and weaken the impact of her message.

15

Here is a 'model' for how Simone could have approached her task. It is all about influencing the attitude of the picking team.

1   It is important for Simone to have the pickers' supervisor on her side, so she should talk to him or her beforehand.

2   She could perhaps ask him or her to introduce the briefing, thus adding extra credibility to the event. This will ensure that Simone has at least one sympathetic listener in the audience.

3   Simone should identify one of the pickers to work on. This should be an **opinion-former** – a person who has a strong influence on the rest of the team. If this person takes a responsible and positive attitude to health and safety issues, even better.

4   She could talk privately to the opinion-former, and convince him or her of her message. She might ask for advice and invite co-operation during the presentation. This should mean a second sympathetic listener.

The next stage is the short briefing itself. Simone should use the connection she has already made with the team supervisor and the 'opinion-former'. She can say things like:

'Sam's already mentioned to me how she . . .'
'. . . and I know Kevin agrees with me . . .'

She can also ask Sam and Kevin to explain or reinforce some points for her. This will help her convince the team. The logic is that this team doesn't start out with any confidence in Simone, but does have confidence in Sam and Kevin. Simone can use this fact to win their acceptance of her messages.

5.4 Demonstrations and briefings

Ordinarily, if you were doing a team briefing, you might want to **demonstrate** rather than just talk.

In the example we have just been discussing, a new method for disposing of waste packing materials might involve the supervisor in:

> Demonstrations are vital: I see and I remember; I do and I understand.

- walking the team round the site, and pointing out examples of good and bad practice;
- demonstrating how to use a machine for compressing waste into bundles – a potentially dangerous machine.

There is a standard formula for this kind of briefing-demonstration:

1. introduce the subject and describe **what** is required;

2. explain **why**;

3. explain **when** the new procedure is to be used;

4. demonstrate **how** to carry out the procedure;

5. ask team members to do it for themselves;

6. correct and advise them where necessary;

7. check understanding and competence;

8. repeat stages 4 to 7 if necessary.

 Portfolio of evidence C12.1, D1.2

Activity 12

 20 mins

This Activity may provide the basis of appropriate evidence for your S/NVQ portfolio. If you are intending to take this course of action, it might be better to write your answers on separate sheets of paper.

Prepare and rehearse an outline for a team briefing based on the formula above. Choose a topic that:

■ is of real importance;
■ requires both an explanation in words and a visual demonstration.

When you are happy with your outline, deliver the briefing. Afterwards, note down briefly how well it worked, and where the problems, if any, lay. Indicate what you will do next time to improve your briefing skills.

A model of influence

This model, with some additions, will prove useful in many situations where a manager, supervisor or team leader is trying to put over a message or a case in the face of disinterest, scepticism or opposition.

It is particularly relevant to meetings, but here you would need to do a little more work beforehand, in particular:

■ sending round papers or memos explaining your case;
■ finding out who might be particularly hostile as well as who might be particularly friendly;

17

- discovering the nature of their objections;
- lobbying – explaining your case and asking for support on a one-to-one basis;
- doing deals – agreeing to support another person's case in return for their supporting yours.

Your preparatory work will help you set out your argument at the meeting itself. You personally will be fully convinced of the wisdom of your proposals, but you need to accept that others may not be.

Try to establish what other people see as the weaknesses of your ideas and the nature of their objections to them. Then address these in your contribution.

> When dealing with possible objections, it pays to 'get your retaliation in first'.

6 Body language

Before human beings discovered how to talk, and long before they discovered how to write, they communicated – like other animals do – using a visual language of physical signals and signs.

6.1 Common signs and signals

Two common signals that we use are:

- nodding the head to show agreement;
- giving the 'thumbs up' to show approval.

Activity 13

4 mins

List **six** or **seven** other signals that we commonly use.

_____

_____

_____

_____

_____

_____

See page 88 for my suggestions.

These are large gestures which we use deliberately as an extension of our ordinary language, or in situations where our voices wouldn't be heard, but body language goes much further than this.

6.2 Unconscious body language

We use a wide range of facial expressions and body movements that reveal our feelings and our reactions to other people. Often we use these signs without consciously intending to. We smile when we're pleased, frown when we're worried, sweat when we're under pressure, and tremble when we're frightened.

We all learn to recognize these signs, which play an important role in social interactions. We can tell by someone's behaviour whether they are excited, bored, tired, mystified, irritated, friendly, hostile, nervous and so on. These signs can provide us with more reliable feedback than a question would.

■ Desmond was briefing some colleagues on his section's reorganization plans. One or two of them looked interested, nodded from time to time and took notes. However, Desmond noticed a couple of others who seemed to spend most of the time doodling, gazing at the posters on the office wall or fiddling with their fingernails.

> **EXTENSION 2**
> Learning to control body language is a key skill for ambitious managers, as this short book points out.

When he'd finished, Desmond looked all round the group and asked 'Does anyone have any questions?' One of the people who'd been taking notes asked a question, but neither of the 'doodlers' did. Desmond made a final attempt to check: 'Is everyone happy?' All those present either nodded agreement or murmured 'yes'. But sure enough, it later turned out that the doodlers hadn't grasped the main point of the reorganization at all. A couple of weeks later Desmond had to brief them all over again.

Activity 14

4 mins

In this case study, Desmond was right about what the doodlers' body language was telling him. What could he have done in the circumstances?

_____

_____

_____

If Desmond was a school teacher, he would probably have put the doodlers on the spot by asking them some searching questions. However, this isn't possible with colleagues.

The alternative would be to make an extra effort to engage their interest, perhaps by:

- making more eye contact with them than with others present;
- making references to how their particular departments or functions might be affected by his plans;
- asking them polite questions relating to this.

6.3 Body language and credibility

Body language sends messages. When these are consistent with the verbal messages we're trying to communicate, there is no problem.

When body language tells a different story, the credibility of the message is weakened. The simplest example of this is when someone tries to make a bold and positive statement, but is too nervous to make eye contact with the audience.

Body language can also distract from the message when it is amusing or irritating. This is particularly true of the mannerisms and 'twitches' that most people seem to adopt when speaking in public. We will have more to say about this in Session C.

Self-assessment 1

1 Communication at work often serves a practical purpose. What is the hidden agenda in all communication?

_____

2 One of these statements is assertive. Which one?

a 'For the last time, will you get those ✳✳✳ boxes away from the fire exit!'

b 'Do you think it might be a good idea to do something about those boxes by the fire exit, perhaps?'

c 'There are some boxes blocking the fire exit. Can you have them removed at once, please.'

3 Fill in the blanks so that these well-known sayings make sense:

I _____ and I forget.

I see _____ and I _____.

I do and I _____.

4 Authority comes from your formal position in the organization, but also from four other things.

We have removed the first two and last two letters from the words that describe them. What are they?

__ __ PERTI __ __

__ __ MPETEN __ __

__ __ IRNE __ __

__ __ NSISTEN __ __

5 Name three digital electronic channels of communication.

_____

_____

_____

6 What do members of teams:

a know _____

b share _____

c possess _____

that members of random groups do not?

7 When you are preparing to argue a case, you should find out the nature of any objections to it beforehand. Why?

_____

_____

8 How can a speaker's body language:

a reduce the speaker's credibility

_____

b weaken the speaker's messages.

_____

Answers to these questions can be found on pages 85–6.

7 Summary

- When managers, supervisors or team leaders speak to colleagues or their team:

  - they **often** do so in order to achieve a particular objective;
  - but they **always** affect working relationships.

- Effective communication has outcomes that change the world in small but useful ways.

- Communication is a two-way process in which attention to feedback is crucial. It always pays to check that the messages have got through.

- For effective communication:

  - repeat the central message at least once;
  - state clearly what you want done, when and by whom;
  - speak clearly and assertively;
  - keep it short and simple;
  - use words and phrases that you are confident the receiver(s) will understand;
  - check that they understand;
  - use visuals to supplement your verbal messages;
  - speak calmly and at a gentle pace;
  - limit the amount of information you try to communicate;
  - make sure your body language matches your message.

- Channels available for communication include writing, face-to-face speech, the telephone and other digital electronic means. The choice of channel depends on the situation:

  - writing is appropriate where messages are longer and more complex, and where they need to go on the record;
  - face-to-face speech is important where credibility, authority and working relationships are at stake.

- Communicating with random groups poses problems, because the speaker doesn't know enough about the group: fortunately most groups are not altogether random.

- Communicating with teams is usually easier, because they share values, trust and understanding. When trying to influence a team it usually pays to begin by convincing the leaders or opinion-formers.

- Team briefings should contain a mixture of verbal explanations and demonstrations. It is important to check understanding and repeat anything that hasn't been understood.

- Body language plays a big role in communication. Make sure that it doesn't distract from or contradict your message.

Session B Meetings

1 Introduction

Meetings may be a pleasure, a necessity, a chore, a nuisance or a test, depending on the circumstances.

They can seem like a waste of valuable time. Certainly meetings take up time; certainly many meetings are badly organized and poorly chaired. They can be inconclusive and frustrating.

Most managers strongly dislike such meetings. Many less experienced managers, supervisors and team leaders loathe **all** meetings.

■ 'Not another stupid meeting!' groaned Anil. 'Why can't we get on with something useful instead of talking about it all the time!'

Anil's line manager put him straight. 'Look, I know you're keen and want to do practical things, but you're moving into management now. Your job is to organize, lead and motivate the people who do the work, not to do the work yourself.'

'We can always replace an operative, but good managers aren't so easy to find. Meetings are a big part of every manager's life and in this company we don't hold meetings for the fun of it. They've always got a practical purpose, and it's time you realized it.'

Meetings are indeed a fact of life: the point is to learn to make them work, both as a participant and when chairing them.

23

2 What meetings are for

Meetings may be **formal** or **informal**. Informal meetings between two or three people take place all the time. You will probably take part in at least one today.

EXTENSION 3
NEBS Management Workbook *Listening and Speaking* deals with clear speaking and making notes.

We are not going to spend much time on informal meetings, but here are three useful rules for every kind of meeting:

■ make your messages clear and simple;
■ listen carefully to what the other person has to say;
■ if anything important was said, make a note of it immediately afterwards.

2.1 Formal meetings

If you work for a very small organization, formal meetings may be few and far between, though even here there is bound to be the occasional meeting with suppliers, the bank, the local authority etc.

In bigger organizations, there are many more meetings, and they play a much more important role in the running of the organization.

Activity 15

4 mins

List the regular formal meetings in which you or your manager take part.

_____
_____
_____
_____
_____
_____

You may have listed some of the following:

'Committee: a body of persons appointed or elected for some special business or purpose.' *Shorter Oxford English Dictionary.*

■ monthly management meeting;
■ production meeting;
■ safety committee;
■ staff association committee;
■ training policy committee;
■ quality circle meetings.

These are all regular meetings, scheduled in advance. There will also be various unscheduled one-off meetings to respond to problems and issues of various kinds.

24

Activity 16

4 mins

Here are some suggestions as to why larger organizations have so many more meetings. Tick any that you think might apply, and add any others that occur to you.

Larger organizations are naturally more bureaucratic. ☐

Larger organizations need formal channels of communication. ☐

Managers in large organizations see meetings as a way of developing their careers. ☐

Many people prefer attending meetings to doing real work. ☐

Other suggestions:

_____

_____

While larger organizations may be bureaucratic, and some managers may see meetings as a way of developing their careers, in general these are not the reasons for having formal meetings. Nor do most organizations tolerate people who would rather attend meetings than do real work. Meetings are work, and often generate work for the people who attend them.

The real answer is the need for communication. In a small organization, everyone knows everyone else. Usually, everyone knows what is going on without needing any formal system of communication.

In larger organizations it is different. People work at different tasks in different departments and even in different locations. While there may be informal networks of contacts that cross these boundaries, they are usually quite limited. They also tend to foster gossip and rumour rather than the communication of information.

So larger organizations – simply because they are large – can't rely on **informal** ways of communicating with and between different groups of staff. They need to establish formal systems and structures.

You may have added some thoughts about **management control**, because this is also more difficult to achieve in larger organizations, for the same reasons.

So we have two good practical reasons for having regular formal meetings:

- for better communication;
- for better management control.

2.2 Meetings for communicating information

All meetings involve a good deal of information, but some meetings take place solely in order to:

- **give information** (as when a manager calls a meeting of staff to announce a plan to move to new offices);
- **get information** (as when a representative from each department is asked to report on developments);
- **exchange information** (as when staff association or union reps from different locations get together).

Consultative meetings – where management wishes to get initial reactions to ideas or proposals – are quite common.

- The management team at Rembrandt Infoproductions Ltd set up a 'consumer group' consisting of typical frequent users of its Internet services. The group met every two months to discuss whatever new services and features the company was thinking of adding. Their role was to help identify those services that were likely to be most – and least – attractive to other users.

2.3 Meetings for management control

Organizations exist to achieve certain goals and objectives, and their day-to-day operations are designed to deliver them. The whole purpose of management is to make sure that this actually happens.

On the one hand, managers create a plan which:

- defines the operations required to meet the objectives;
- identifies the resources needed to carry out the operations;
- sets targets for all relevant activities.

On the other hand, they design systems which compare what actually happens with the plan:

- **monitoring** and **measuring** activities and use of resources;
- **reviewing** progress against targets;
- if necessary **modifying** future operations in the light of this.

This is known as a **control cycle**, and **review meetings** are a central part of it. As you can see, it is all about information. In fact, we can also think of meetings of this kind as **systems for processing information**.

■ Abraxis is a charity that helps handicapped children. The management team meets monthly to review activities and budgets. A few days before the meeting, participants are sent two main documents. One summarizes the activities of various projects. The other summarizes revenue and costs and compares them with budgets. The meeting concentrates on dealing with areas where there is a significant deviation from the plans, targets and budgets, such as:

  ■ projects failing to achieve their targets;
  ■ revenue shortfalls;
  ■ excess costs.

The meeting will discuss these points, and try to establish:

  ■ whether the deviations really are significant;
  ■ what the consequences will be if they are not corrected;
  ■ what needs to be done to correct them;
  ■ who will take responsibility for ensuring that it happens;
  ■ how and when this will be in turn be reviewed.

Activity 17

This control process begins with information, and there are four more elements in the control cycle. Write a word or two in each of the boxes below to show what they are.

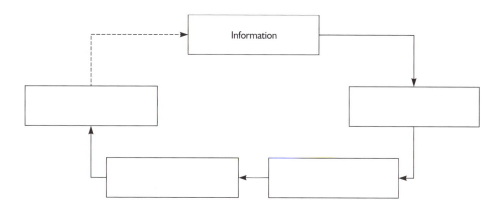

See page 88 for my suggestions.

Activity 18

20 mins

This Activity may provide the basis of appropriate evidence for your S/NVQ portfolio. If you are intending to take this course of action, it might be better to write your answers on separate sheets of paper.

The Activities of your own team are no doubt monitored and controlled in a similarly structured way. Find out about what happens at a typical review meeting where activities, budgets and progress are discussed. If possible take part in one yourself (you may need to get permission for this).

Outline and explain:

- what information about operations is examined in the meeting;
- how the progress of operations is reviewed;
- what action is taken to modify future operations, if any;
- how the results of the action will themselves be monitored.

Does the meeting have a fair picture of what is happening on the ground? Could you help make that picture more accurate by providing more or different information?

Every organization does things slightly differently, but the odds are that yours uses a control cycle similar to that described in Activity 17. However, you may well have felt that the meeting did not have an accurate picture of your team's work and the issues facing you.

This may be partly because of a difference of perspective: higher levels of management see issues more broadly and are less concerned with detail. Nevertheless, you might be able to improve the quality of information about your activities.

Bear in mind that higher levels of management don't want:

- excuses for why you didn't meet your targets;
- more information than they can readily digest.

We can now sum up the uses of meetings:

- they are an important channel for the communication of information;
- they play a central part in the cycle of management control;
- except in very small organizations, meetings are a convenient and practical method of achieving these things.

2.4 Problems with meetings

There are two problems with meetings:

- first, they use up **resources** – mainly the time of key personnel – and that therefore they have a cost;
- second, they **can** be badly handled, resulting in a **waste** of resources.

Activity 19

4 mins

Think back to some poor meetings that you have attended. Jot down **eight** or **ten** words that describe what you felt was wrong with them.

_____   _____
_____   _____
_____   _____
_____   _____
_____

We have all experienced bad meetings, so I expect you chose words which described how unhappy you were at:

- having to deal with trivial issues;
- having to attend meetings that had nothing serious to discuss;
- having to spend long periods in meetings that weren't of much relevance to your own work.

- In his book _The Law and the Profits_, C. Northcote Parkinson describes a company board meeting in which the members spend hours wrangling about a proposal to spend £500 on a new lawnmower, while a major investment costing millions of pounds goes through in a matter of minutes. The explanation, says Parkinson, is that everyone present understands lawnmowers, and has something sensible to say. Only one or two of those present understand the big investment proposal, and the rest don't feel they have anything sensible to say at all.

You may also have attended meetings that were unfocused, badly chaired or dominated by argument between warring factions. Meetings that go on too long, that drift off into digressions, or fail to reach conclusions are also very irritating.

29

It's also irritating when a meeting is allowed to drift on to its maximum allotted time when it could easily be wrapped up early. It's annoying when some individuals are allowed to speak at enormous length while others never seem to get a word in.

However, meetings do not have to be like this. As we will show, meetings can be efficient, productive and even enjoyable – provided that:

■ they are well organized;
■ and well chaired;
■ and that the participants behave sensibly.

Preparation is an important part of this: people who go to meetings without proper preparation not only put less in, they take less out.

3 Preparing for a meeting

There are two sides to this:

■ how the organizer prepares;
■ how the participants prepare.

3.1 How to organize a meeting

It is worth producing a checklist which you can run through every time you have to organize a meeting until it becomes second nature.

Activity 20

You have been asked to attend a consultative meeting about proposed changes in the way staff holiday entitlement is organized. The meeting is organized by Deanne, the company secretary.

What would you expect Deanne to do to help the participants prepare for the meeting?

_____

_____

_____

_____

There are some obvious practical issues. For example, the participants need to know where and when the meeting will take place. Even before this, Deanne should probably check individually with the participants to find out whether they can actually attend on the proposed dates.

This is often a major administrative problem with one-off meetings. Everyone is busy, some people will be away, others will have prior commitments they cannot break. The more people are required to attend, the harder the task becomes. This is why the dates of routine meetings are often booked a long time in advance.

You will probably also expect Deanne to send you:

- a list of who else is expected to attend;
- any documents relating to the matter to be discussed – including the new proposal itself, extracts from existing contracts of employment, memos on the subject by senior people, and so on;
- an agenda.

Agendas are simply a list of the items to be discussed, but, as we will see a little later, they can play a vital role in ensuring that a meeting goes well.

Activity 21

Still on the subject of the meeting about holiday entitlement, how would you prepare yourself for this meeting?

_____

_____

_____

_____

Again there are practical issues. You should, for instance:

- note where and when the meeting is to be, and mark it in your diary or on your wall chart;
- allow yourself enough time to get to the meeting before it starts.

The next part of preparation is to read the documentation. If you don't understand all or part of it, ask someone to explain. Don't leave this to the meeting itself.

Finally, prepare your contribution to the meeting. If the matter is not confidential, you could discuss it with your team. It may be useful to take their views to the meeting. You should certainly discuss it informally with colleagues, as there may well be implications that you were not aware of.

If you intend to make a contribution, make brief notes in advance. That way, your part in the meeting will be both briefer and more effective.

3.2 Practical arrangements

Like any other work activity, meetings should take place in suitable physical conditions.

■ Robin's manager asked her to deputize for him at a meeting called by the IT department to explain some forthcoming developments in information technology. The meeting took place on a Friday afternoon. The weather was hot and the sun shone relentlessly through the windows of the stuffy training room where the meeting took place. Several people tried to open windows, but they were fixed tight by security bolts.

It was impossible to concentrate on the speaker. After 15 minutes, Robin had to pinch herself to keep awake. From behind her she heard the gentle snores of the security manager.

Activity 22

4 mins

Poor arrangements mean poor results. Think back over meetings that you have attended. List **five** aspects of the physical arrangements that could have been better.

_____

_____

_____

_____

_____

In meetings, most people spend most of the time listening – and this is something that most humans are not very good at. We generally find it harder to concentrate on someone else talking than on speaking ourselves.

Anything which makes it **more** difficult to listen should be avoided. This includes any location that is:

■ too hot;
■ too noisy;
■ too cramped;
■ too uncomfortable.

> Many a meeting has been disrupted by repeated 'wrong number' telephone calls.

Distractions can also be a problem. Pagers and mobile phones should be switched off, and even telephone extensions might be unplugged.

People with no business at the meeting should be encouraged to keep away. A notice on the door should read:

> MEETING IN PROGRESS

Layout

The layout of the chairs and tables at a meeting is also of some importance. For example, in some meetings everyone sits at a long table arranged like this:

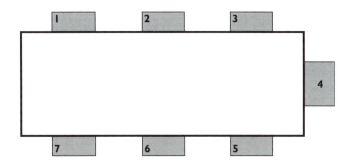

Activity 23

4 mins

There are seven seats here. Which one will the chairman sit in? _____

Where will the next two most important people sit? _____

Why might it be a bad idea to adopt a seating arrangement that points to strong differences in status?

_____

_____

In this traditional 'baronial table' layout, the chairman – who will sit at the head of the table in seat 4 (a larger seat than the others) – is obviously given a higher status than everyone else. The next most important individuals will probably sit next to him or her in seats 3 and 5.

Such an arrangement puts the people who sit in seats 1 and 7 at a disadvantage. Their visibly lower status puts them under pressure. They may find it harder to make eye contact with the chairman, and may feel too intimidated to make the contributions that they would like to make.

Since one point of bringing people together for a meeting is to draw on useful contributions from all of them, this is counter-productive. Whatever the intentions of the organizers, it is an authoritarian layout. It does not suggest a group of people capable of working together as a team.

Activity 24

Here is another layout that is often used for meetings.

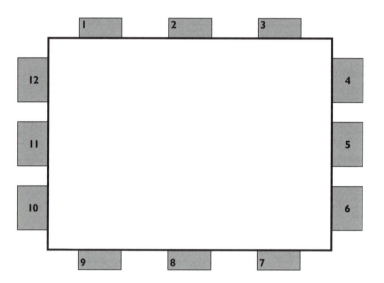

There are 12 seats, but only nine people are at the meeting.

Which seats will be unoccupied? _____

Where will the chairman sit? _____

What does this layout say about the status of the various people taking part?

_____

_____

This is a perfectly practical layout for a meeting, but it doesn't have any implications for status. It doesn't matter where anyone sits, including the chairman – in fact it is a modern version of King Arthur's Round Table, which was specifically designed to avoid disputes over status.

When managers, supervisors and team leaders organize meetings with their team, this kind of layout is usually appropriate. It may simply consist of a circle of chairs.

Activity 25

Finally, here is another quite different kind of layout.

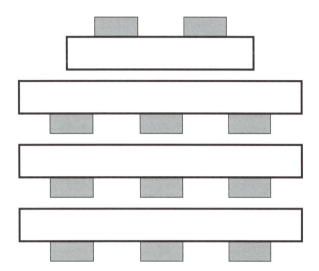

What comment would you make about this seating arrangement?

_____

_____

_____

_____

This layout is not suitable for a meeting of the kinds we have been discussing. It is more like a 'speaker-audience' setup. It tells us that someone is going to sit or perhaps stand at the front and make announcements or a presentation to the rest of those present. The layout encourages them to be passive listeners, rather than to participate – though they may be able to ask questions at the end.

3.3 The agenda

The agenda is a programme for what will happen at the meeting. It lists the main points that will be under discussion, plus some administrative details.

It therefore:

Participants may be asked in advance whether they want anything put on the agenda.

- tells the participants what will be discussed;
- gives the chairman a framework for managing the meeting.

Here is a typical agenda for the monthly meeting of a voluntary organization's Development Group.

**DEVELOPMENT GROUP
MONTHLY MEETING**

3 October 199X
3.30pm in the Tavistock Centre

AGENDA

1 Apologies for absence.

2 Minutes of the last meeting.

3 Matters arising

4 Launch of Jubilee Fields Project.

5 Other possible projects.

6 Funding.

7 Any other business.

8 Date of next meeting.

The first three items are standard for regular meetings that are fairly formal and where **minutes** are taken.

Minutes

Minutes provide a permanent record of who was there, what was said and what decisions were taken. However, they are not verbatim transcripts of what was said – that would take too long to type up and would be too tedious to read. Instead, minutes should record formal details of:

- who attended the meeting;
- what topics were discussed;
- what decisions were taken;
- what action, when and by whom, should follow.

Under each major topic they should provide a concise summary of:

- the key points made by various contributors;
- the main arguments for and against any decision.

■ The Board of Trustees of the charity Abraxis meets every four or five weeks. The Deputy Chief Executive is responsible for the minutes. He makes detailed notes in the course of the meeting, and edits them later.

Unfortunately, this is treated as a low-priority task. Typically, the minutes of the previous meeting do not reach participants until a few days before the next one.

Activity 26

4 mins

This delay in typing up and distributing minutes could cause problems. Why do you think this might be?

_____

_____

If the meeting is just a 'talking shop', then it might not matter that the minutes go out very late. But if decisions are taken, and individuals are asked to act on them, it is a very different story: the decisions may not be implemented, and the actions may not be taken, until much later than intended.

There's another reason for wishing to have minutes sooner rather than later. They are a permanent record, but there may well be mistakes or omissions. Agenda item 2 *Minutes of the last meeting* is an opportunity to correct these for the record.

Matters arising

This agenda item gives participants a chance to bring the meeting up to date on matters discussed last time.

This should not be an invitation to go over the subject a second time: only significant new information will be welcome here.

Any other business?

This can be one of the big problem areas in formal meetings.

■ The meeting had spent two hours working through a number of issues to do with health and safety. Everyone had had enough, and was ready to go home. 'Right then', said the chairman. 'Any other business?'

'Yes chairman', said Winston. 'I would like to bring to your attention a serious matter that arose just a few days ago ...' He proceeded to read out a long letter from a member of the public whose child had had a minor accident on one of the council's sports fields.

'Ruts in the sports fields are quite a hazard', continued Winston. 'I would like to know what is being done about them, what warnings are being given to the public, and what other incidents have occurred. And I don't think this is a matter that we can put off ...'

Activity 27

4 mins

The meeting is now going to run over time, perhaps significantly. If you were the chairman of this meeting, what would you do?

_____

_____

By raising a complicated issue under 'Any other business', Winston risks making himself very unpopular. Assuming the issue really is important, what should he have done?

_____

_____

What happens under 'Any other business' (AOB) is usually up to the meeting, though the chairman will have a big influence over events. There may be **standing orders** – rules for running the meetings – stating that important topics may not be discussed under AOB. If not, and if the others present at the meeting indicate that they do not want to deal with the matter, the chairman may:

■ refuse to allow any discussion on this subject;
■ remit (postpone) it until the next meeting;
■ appoint a sub-group to deal with it.

If a genuinely important matter crops up at the last minute, the meeting may have to deal with it, whether they want to or not.

In this case, however, Winston is clearly at fault. Since he knew about this matter well in advance of the meeting, he should have contacted the chairman or the committee secretary and asked for the item to be put on the agenda.

The very last item on an agenda is usually setting the date of the next meeting.

The documents could then have been distributed in advance and the other participants could have prepared themselves properly.

4 Chairing a meeting

It is possible for a meeting to work without someone being 'in the chair' – but an effective chairperson can make a tremendous difference to the efficiency of the proceedings.

The chairperson's role is to control and guide the meeting to ensure that it achieves its objectives. He or she will be expected to ensure that:

- the formalities are dealt with correctly;
- the topics on the agenda are adequately covered in the time available;
- everyone with something useful to say has an opportunity to say it;
- no-one speaks for too long;
- everyone keeps to the point;
- decisions are reached by agreement and are fully understood.

The chairperson's authority to do these things may be based on standing orders, but it won't work unless those present at the meeting consent to it being handled that way.

Portfolio of evidence D1.1, D1.2

Activity 28

20 mins

This Activity may provide the basis of appropriate evidence for your S/NVQ portfolio. If you are intending to take this course of action, it might be better to write your answers on separate sheets of paper.

In order to carry out this Activity you will need to be present at at least one formal meeting for which an agenda and minutes are usually produced. If you are not normally invited to such meetings, ask your manager to obtain permission for you to do so.

The aim is to observe and comment on how the chairperson operates. Watch and listen throughout the meeting and take notes.

After the meeting, write a brief description of how the chairperson:

1　introduced the meeting and got it started;

2　managed the agenda, to ensure all the important points were covered in the time available;

3　ensured that everyone had the opportunity to contribute;

4　controlled individual speakers, to keep them brief and to the point;

5　brought the meeting to a close.

Score the chairperson out of ten for each of these five points, and explain briefly what the problems were, if any.

When meetings are unsatisfactory it isn't necessarily the chairperson's fault. Sometimes urgent issues crop up at the last minute, and the agenda has to be abandoned. Sometimes it is simply impossible to reach a conclusion on one or more agenda items.

■ One item on the Board's agenda was improvements to security, following a series of break-ins and acts of vandalism. A junior member of the management team had been asked to get advice from security firms, to propose new security measures, and to establish their cost and effectiveness.

The proposals made sense in practical terms, but the cost was much higher than the Board was prepared to accept. After a long discussion, the meeting appointed a sub-committee to draw up revised proposals within an agreed cost limit. They were given two weeks to do so, and the Managing Director was authorized to take an immediate decision as soon as she had seen their report.

Meetings revolve around information. They can't come to a sensible conclusion or make good decisions if the information before them is:

A final note for chairpeople: resist the temptation to do too much talking yourself.

■ incomplete;
■ unreliable;
■ inadequate.

The quality of information before the meeting is partly the responsibility of the organizers, but the contributors also share this responsibility.

5 Making your contribution

It is not enough just to turn up at a meeting and leave all the preparation to the organizer.

5.1 Responsible contributions

Contributors share the responsibility for how well meetings work.

Activity 29

4 mins

What can a responsible contributor do to make sure a meeting goes well? Suggest **three** or **four** guidelines.

_____

_____

_____

_____

In general, contributors to a meeting should take a positive and constructive attitude. They should share the chairperson's objective of trying to get through the agenda in good time and reach sensible conclusions.

A passive or hostile attitude, which often comes from people who 'hate meetings', certainly won't improve matters.

The other points for contributors are:

- study the documents in advance;
- if there's any matter that you don't understand, seek clarification before the meeting starts;
- make your contributions brief and effective.

The meeting is not the place for asking basic questions like 'What is this project, then?' or 'How do we know that there is a demand for this product?'

5.2 Effective contributions

When you attend a meeting, you may make a contribution for one of several reasons. You may:

- be responsible for introducing or proposing an agenda item (sometimes called 'talking to' the item);
- take part in a discussion, voicing your opinions, explaining your views and arguing your case;
- ask questions;
- provide answers to other people's questions.

There are three reasons why you should try to make good-quality contributions to a meeting:

- it will help the meeting work better and produce better outcomes;
- you are more likely to achieve the outcomes you are personally seeking;
- it will improve your personal reputation and help your career.

But what is a 'good-quality' contribution?

Activity 30

Write down **six** words that would describe a good-quality contribution.

_____   _____

_____   _____

_____   _____

You probably listed words like relevant, coherent, brief, powerful, well-informed, well-argued, and so on. Actually the measure of quality is when listeners think to themselves 'That made a lot of sense', showing that the messages got through, and were both understandable and credible.

We can split the success factors here for effective contributions to meetings into three groups.

STRUCTURAL FACTORS	include:	
	a beginning	in which you outline what you are going to say and why
	a middle	in which you explain the detail of your ideas
	an end	in which you sum up your case
	logical links	so that the whole thing makes sense
CONTENT FACTORS	be relevant	focus clearly on the topic and address your own objectives
	be factual	back up your ideas with information, references, case studies etc.
	be brief	keep it short, avoid digressions
DELIVERY FACTORS	manner	be calm, reasonable and polite but assertive – this makes listeners more receptive
	style	use simple and straightforward language – this helps the message get through
	voice	speak clearly and loud enough for everyone to hear – this also suggests confidence
	visuals	use tables, graphs, pictures etc. to support your case
	body language	make eye contact all around the room – avoid distracting mannerisms and gestures

Of course this advice applies mainly to longer contributions. Session C, which deals with presentations, goes into these issues in more detail. Most of your contributions at meetings will be fairly brief. All the more reason to keep them simple and straightforward.

When to speak

Inevitably there is an element of game playing about meetings. During a discussion, some people deliberately try to make their mark early. Others like to lie low until the end of the discussion, and then to ambush everyone else with a powerful and conclusive statement. Some people feel that they should try to speak as often as possible, whether or not they have anything sensible to say.

Research suggests that people who speak too often, too long and too late in a discussion lose credibility in the eyes of others.

The best strategy seems to be:

- to make your first contribution fairly early in a discussion;
- to listen to what others have to say;
- return to the subject when you have a reasoned response to make.

6 Negotiations

Like meetings, negotiations can be either formal or informal.

- Louise asked one of her team – Nico – to take part in a market research project that would involve him in about 10 hours work a week for seven weeks. Nico was interested, but pointed out that being on the project would mean 10 hours a week less in which to do his normal job.

  Louise expected this. Her response was to offer Nico some extra clerical help, but Nico felt that this would still leave him about five hours a week short.

  Louise suggested that Nico could probably cope with this. Nico was still reluctant.

  Louise pointed out that being on the market research project would be a useful career move for Nico. Nico agreed and thanked Louise for the opportunity but said he was still concerned about the additional pressure and the possibility of his normal work falling behind.

  The two colleagues considered several options.

  Louise finally bridged the gap by agreeing to transfer one of Nico's routine tasks to another colleague, Grace, for the duration of the project, on condition that Nico spent a reasonable amount of time training and briefing Grace in how to do it.

This kind of 'dealing', which goes on a lot at work, is a classic example of negotiation. Other negotiations may be formal, as when:

- discussing changes to pay and conditions with union or staff association representatives;
- seeking an agreement with suppliers or customers over contract terms or compensation for poor work;
- agreeing the terms for a collaborative venture.

Negotiations have five main characteristics in common:

- there is a **gap** to be bridged between two (and sometimes more) positions;
- both sides recognize that it is desirable to reach an **agreement**;
- both sides are willing to make **concessions** in order to reach agreement;
- neither side knows in advance **how much** the other is willing to concede;
- the negotiation process consists of repeated **exchanges of messages**.

The outcome of a negotiation should be a decision which is, in the circumstances, satisfactory to both sides.

Usually this means a compromise of some kind. Typically, each side enters the negotiation recognizing that they may not get everything they want. On the other hand, each will have a limit beyond which they are not willing to go.

> Both sides in a negotiation should set themselves SMART objectives:
>
> **S** pecific
> **M** easurable
> **A** chievable
> **R** ealistic
> **T** imed.

- Randolph Provisions were negotiating the price on the purchase of corned beef from a new supplier. Their buyer was prepared to pay a maximum of 39p per 340 g tin for 22,000 packs of 24 tins, but her objective was to get the price down to 35p. The supplier's salesman was prepared to accept a minimum of 37p, but was aiming to achieve 41p. However, he would accept a slightly lower price if the order quantity was higher.

Activity 31

3 mins

The two negotiators can reach agreement across a range of prices.

What is the maximum price in this range? _____

What is the minimum price in this range? _____

What might enable the buyer to achieve a lower price?

_____

_____

The range within which the agreed price will fall is the area where the buyer's and the supplier's maximum and minimum prices overlap. We can show this **negotiable area** in a table, like this, with a dash indicating a price that one side is not prepared to consider:

buyer's range:	35	36	37	38	39	–	–
supplier's range:	–	–	37	38	39	40	41

The price range is therefore between 37p and 39p, but remember that neither side actually knows where the other's maximum and minimum lie.

It is up to the two negotiators to use their skills to try to persuade each other in the direction of the most favourable outcome for themselves. Above 39p and below 37p, agreement is of course not possible.

What happens if there is a log-jam – for example if the buyer refuses to go above 36p? The supplier might agree to shift his minimum price downwards if:

■ the buyer increased the order quantity;
■ the buyer agreed a longer-term contract;
■ the buyer agreed to take some other produce from the supplier as well.

Activity 32

2 mins

Highlight the square in this matrix which should represent the best outcome of a negotiation.

Outcome as perceived by
Side B

	Win	Lose
Win	Win – Win	Win – Lose
Lose	Lose – Win	Lose – Lose

Outcome as perceived by Side A

It may seem tempting for one side to win and the other to lose, but this often proves counter-productive:

- if one side has clearly 'lost' the agreement it may be repudiated by more senior people on that side;
- a losing negotiator may feel resentful, and may seek revenge at some later date.

The best outcome is where both sides perceive themselves as winning. Naturally a result in which neither side wins is an outright failure.

Negotiation skills are valuable and take time to learn, and we can't go into much detail here. Two additional points are worth including, though.

First, successful negotiations depend on both sides paying very careful attention to what the other side is saying. In order to get a precise understanding, they need to ask each other many kinds of questions, for example:

Reflecting	*So what you're saying is . . .*
Supporting	*Yes, that's a very positive suggestion. So can we . . .*
Disagreeing	*Won't that cost too much?*
Constructing	*Would it help if . . .?*
Clarifying	*Isn't the point that . . .?*
Interpreting	*Are you suggesting . . .?*
Confirming	*So we agree that . . .*
Testing	*Would it be right to say that . . .?*

Second, agreements may be complex and contain a lot of detail. It is extremely important to write down and agree these details before breaking up the meeting.

All in all, clear messages and accurate understanding are absolutely vital to a successful negotiation. Poor communicators will soon find themselves in difficulties.

Self-assessment 2

12 mins

1 Define 'committee'.

_____

_____

2 Regular formal meetings are held within organizations for two main purposes. What are they?

a _____

b _____

47

3   What do we mean by 'a control cycle'?

_____

_____

4   What **three** things should participants in a meeting do to ensure they are thoroughly prepared?

a   _____

b   _____

c   _____

5   Chairing a meeting is a position of power, even if it is only temporary. What temptation must the chairperson try to resist?

The temptation to: _____

6   Seating arrangements at a meeting have significance. Why?

_____

_____

7   Comment briefly on these statements about meetings.

a   The agenda should be flexible and participants should be able to add items if they wish.

_____

_____

b   Minutes should record the proceedings in as much detail as possible.

_____

_____

c   People not saying enough is as big a problem as people saying too much.

_____

_____

8   If one side clearly loses in a negotiation, what risks are being run?

a   _____

b   _____

Answers to these questions can be found on pages 86–7.

7 Summary

- All formal meetings at work involve giving, getting, and exchanging information, and some take place solely for that purpose.

- Others are primarily designed for management control:
  - **monitoring** and **measuring** activities and use of resources;
  - **reviewing** progress against targets;
  - if necessary **modifying** future operations in the light of this.

- Meetings are therefore both necessary and useful, but there can be problems. All meetings use resources of time, and bad meetings waste them.

- Organizers, chairmen and participants share a responsibility for making meetings work.

- Practical arrangements are important:
  - arranging suitable dates;
  - sending out agendas and documents;
  - ensuring the location and seating plans are suitable.

- Participants should prepare by:
  - reading the documents;
  - getting clarification in advance about anything that is unclear to them;
  - thinking about the issues and perhaps discussing them with others;
  - making notes about the contributions they intend to make.

- The agenda lays down the programme for the meeting, though this can be amended if necessary. Minutes summarize the who, what and why of the discussions, and report on the action that is to follow.

- The chairperson of a meeting is responsible for ensuring that:
  - the formalities are dealt with correctly;
  - the topics on the agenda are adequately covered in the time available;
  - everyone with something useful to say has an opportunity to say it;
  - no one speaks for too long;
  - everyone keeps to the point;
  - decisions are reached by agreement and are fully understood.

- Contributions should be brief, to the point and well-structured to ensure that the messages get through.

- Negotiations are a specialized kind of meeting. They depend heavily on clear communication and accurate understanding. Negotiators typically question one another closely, and repeat and summarize ideas in order to ensure that they have not misunderstood one another.

- The most desirable outcome of a negotiation is one where both sides feel happy – a WIN–WIN situation. If one side clearly loses it can cause problems. The outcome is therefore usually a compromise in which both sides concede something.

- The agreements reached at negotiations need to be recorded with care.

Session C Speaking in public

1 Introduction

If you are anything like me, you greatly admire people who can stand up confidently in front of a room full of strangers and deliver a punchy speech.

How come they are so good at it? How come they don't tremble and stutter with nerves? How do they manage to make everything they say seem so important and convincing?

It is tempting to think that they are a totally different kind of person from you and me – that they are 'born public speakers'.

However, there is no such thing as a 'born public speaker'. Effective speaking is something of which we are all capable, but which we have to learn. It is simply not true that regular speech-makers like the leaders of the big political parties had that skill from birth. I am sure that when they first started they were as nervous as you or me, and suffered their fair share of disasters and humiliations.

So what makes them different? Only three things:

- they were determined to speak;
- they practised a lot;
- they learned the necessary skills.

2 Dealing with nerves

Almost everybody feels nervous when they speak in public. Successful speakers find a way of dealing with it.

2.1 Why we feel nervous

There are several situations in which you may be called on to deliver a speech, a presentation or a talk, for example:

- making a speech at the retirement party of someone from your workteam;
- giving colleagues or management a formal presentation about a project you have been working on;
- briefing a group of visitors about some aspect of your work;
- stating a case at a tribunal or before a committee of some sort.

51

All these situations:

- are fairly formal;
- are fairly important;
- need to be taken seriously;
- place a lot of responsibility on the speaker.

This means that the speaker is under some pressure, and may feel anxious.

- A friend of mine recently described how he felt the first time he had to speak in front of a big audience. He was reading the lesson at school assembly:

'I felt very nervous beforehand. My head was sort of swimming, and somehow I couldn't see properly – everything was a blur. My heart was thumping away like mad. I started off in a great rush and gabbled like an idiot. My voice was all wobbly and I kept having to swallow because my throat was so dry.

'Then when I had settled down a bit I suddenly realized that my left leg was trembling uncontrollably, and I thought everyone must be able to see it. Then I got really nervous. I lost my place, stuttered and started sweating all over. I don't really know how I got through to the end at all.

'When I'd finished I just wanted to run away and hide. I thought I'd be the laughing stock of the whole school. But the funny thing was that no one seemed to mind, and the deputy head actually said 'Well done – but take it a little slower next time.'

Sweating, trembling, racing heart, dry throat, shaking limbs – these are the physical symptoms of severe anxiety, or in other words, fear.

Fear, whether it is mild (feeling nervous) or severe (feeling terrified) is the body's physical response to danger, or the threat of danger. It warns us not to get into danger, but if we do get into danger, it gets us physically ready to run for our lives – or fight for them. Unfortunately, we often experience fear when there isn't any serious physical danger at all – before making a speech in public, for example.

2.2 Controlling anxiety

The anxiety/fear reaction is automatic. However, in practice, we can learn to cope:

- by learning to control our physical reactions;
- by becoming less sensitive to the 'threat';
- by recognizing that the 'threat' itself is not serious;
- by improving our speaking techniques, and thus our self-confidence.

Activity 33

2 mins

Many of us react to having to speak in public as if we were under physical threat. What exactly do you think speakers are afraid of?

_____

_____

Strange as it may seem, it is mainly the thought of making fools of ourselves which makes us react almost as if we were walking into a tiger-infested jungle. On a rational level, those people out there are not really going to do us any harm at all.

So obviously, the first step in controlling your anxiety is to keep telling yourself:

'However bad I may feel right now, I'm not going to die, or be mauled, or be chased through the forest by a tiger. I will easily survive this experience.'

Unfortunately, fear isn't rational, and simply telling yourself these things will not be enough. You also need to learn how to control your reactions.

Activity 34

3 mins

Think for a moment of somebody you have heard giving a speech whom you realized was nervous. Perhaps it was somebody at work, at a wedding or a public meeting.

Jot down what signs the speaker gave that he or she was nervous when starting to speak.

_____

_____

Well, the ways of showing nervousness are endless. But common signs are:

> Relaxation puts the chemical flows created by anxiety into reverse, and it is easy to learn.

- fiddling nervously with tie, cufflinks, jewellery, hair, papers;
- frequent throat-clearing;
- perspiring;
- trembling hands;
- voice too high-pitched, trembling, or not coming out at all.

53

EXTENSION 4
We don't have room here to go into breathing and voice control in detail, but you may like to read this short summary on p. 82.

EXTENSION 5
Learning to relax can be useful in many situations. If you have problems with stress and anxiety, this extension may well help you.

Here are some simple hints for coping with the physical symptoms of anxiety:

- give yourself time: walk a few metres to where you are to speak;
- give yourself time: spend a few seconds arranging your papers before you start;
- clench your fists very tightly, and then relax them as slowly as you can, several times;
- do breathing and voice control exercises;
- learn relaxation techniques.

2.3 Reducing your sensitivity

When someone pops a paper bag behind you, you tend to jump. This is an automatic fear reaction. Some people jump more than others, but basically we all react the same way.

But what happens if someone pops a paper bag behind you every few minutes throughout the day? Answer – gradually your reactions become less violent, until eventually you take no notice at all.

Quite simply, you get used to it. What was a 'threat' the first time becomes less of a threat the second time, until in the end it stops being a threat altogether. In medical terms, you become **desensitized**.

Activity 35

2 mins

Suggest how you could desensitize yourself to the 'threat' posed by having to speak in public.

_____

_____

You cannot overcome anxiety without facing up to it; if you avoid it, it will only get worse.

The answer should be fairly obvious from the paper-bag example:

- you need plenty of exposure to the threat:
- practice and experience will make you less anxious.

Everyone who has to speak in public finds that although it may be bad the first time, the second time it will be better, and so on.

3 Competence and confidence

The other main way to reduce the fear of speaking in public is to increase your confidence that you can do it competently.

Activity 36

3 mins

Suppose you have to make a presentation in a few weeks' time. Note down **two** things that you could do between now and then to build up your confidence.

_____

_____

Anything which helps you make a competent and effective presentation will make you feel more confident on the day, especially:

- careful planning and preparation;
- practising your technique.

3.1 Planning and preparation

If you have prepared your presentation thoroughly, you have every reason to feel confident on the day. But you must be prepared to put in the effort – most speakers find that they spend **at least five times longer** preparing a talk than they actually take to deliver it.

A formula for preparing a presentation or speech

Stage 1: objectives

Think about your purpose, the needs of your listeners, and the context in which you will be speaking.

- Why are you speaking?
- Who will be listening?
- Where will you be speaking?

Stage 2: content

Decide the key points you need to put across to your listeners in order to achieve your objectives.

Stage 3: structure

Work out a sensible and logical structure for the points you are going to make, with a beginning (an introduction), a middle (the main part of the presentation) and an end (summary and conclusions).

Stage 4: visual aids

Select and prepare the diagrams, slides, models and equipment that will help your listeners get the message.

Stage 5: notes

Make a brief outline of what you are going to say, to guide you and make sure you don't miss anything out.

Stage 6: rehearsal

Practise your delivery and make sure that you know how long you will take, how fast to go, and what words to use.

Portfolio of evidence C1.1, C1.2

Activity 37

6 mins

This Activity may provide the basis of appropriate evidence for your S/NVQ portfolio. If you are intending to take this course of action, it might be better to write your answers on separate sheets of paper.

■ Suppose you have to give a presentation to a group of local secondary school teachers who are considering placing work experience students with you. They want to know what it is like to work in your team, and the sort of work you actually do. The presentation will take place at the Teachers' Centre, and you will have up to 15 minutes altogether, plus a little time for questions.

List the key points you would want to make (stage 2 in our formula):

_____

_____

_____

_____

_____

_____

_____

_____

Draft out an introduction and a brief summary and conclusion.

_____

_____

_____

_____

_____

_____

_____

_____

_____

_____

3.2 Visual aids

Why they work

There are three excellent reasons for using visual aids:

I hear and I forget.
I see and I remember.
I do and I understand.

- some things are easier to communicate visually than in speech;
- they help your listeners remember the points you are making;
- they make the whole presentation more interesting and credible.

Activity 38

What sort of visual aids would be useful in a presentation about your own work? Note down **four** different examples.

_____

_____

_____

_____

I don't know what work you do, so I can only make general points, but if I were you, I would ask myself how I could show the audience:

- what the working environment is like (slides, photos, perhaps a video?);
- what our 'end product' is (actual examples, models, photos?);
- what the work we do consists of (diagrams, charts, videos?);
- how the workload, output etc. have progressed (diagrams, charts, videos?).

57

Visual aids don't have to be 'pictorial', of course. One of the most useful things to do is to 'flash up' your key points in writing as you go along – on a flip chart, or as slides for an overhead projector (OHP).

For example, if your first key point is 'This firm has always had a reputation for quality', then present it on the OHP or flip-chart page like this:

---

1   A REPUTATION FOR QUALITY

EXTENSION 6
For a brief guide to using overhead projectors and other modern visual aids, see this summary on p. 83.

You could keep that point on view until you were ready to make the next one. Alternatively, you could put all your points on one sheet or slide and talk through them one by one.

Visual aids are extremely useful, but they need careful preparation, so make sure you allow yourself enough time. Good visual aids can make your presentation go better, but if your visual aids are torn, scruffy, smudged and hard to see, it will go worse.

Checking before you begin

Proper preparation means checking and re-checking:

- check all your visual aids are ready;
- check all the equipment is working properly.

Remember: competence leads to confidence!

---

4 Drafting your speech

You will need to **expand and explain** your key points.

For example, if your first point is that your organization has 'a reputation for quality', you may want to back that up by stating:

- who thinks so;
- what you mean by quality;
- why it is considered important;
- what you do to maintain it.

Let's work out a way of putting down the content of a presentation, using the example I have already given. Here is a reminder of what it involves:

■ You have to give a presentation to a group of local secondary teachers who are considering placing work experience students with you. They want to know what it is like to work in your team, and the sort of work you actually do. The presentation will take place at the Teachers' Centre, and you will have up to 15 minutes altogether, plus a little time for questions.

4.1 Listing the key points

Now let's look at developing the main message.

Activity 39

Look back to your response to Activity 37 and, building on that, think carefully about what you need to say, and then write down the main points here, in logical order, as briefly as you can. Choose no more than **eight** key points.

_____

_____

_____

_____

_____

_____

_____

_____

Obviously you have thought about the logic of what you want to say and it makes sense to you. However, it might be worth checking that they will make sense to your likely audience – perhaps a colleague would help.

When you are happy with your list of key points, write each one at the top of a blank sheet of paper (or a large file card). These will be the skeleton of your presentation.

4.2 Listing the subsidiary points

Now we go through a process of refining the key points to include everything else we need to say.

Activity 40

15 mins

Consider each of your key points in turn and think about what you will want to say about each. Under each one, list the main things you will want to say, making sure to put them in a logical order.

For example:

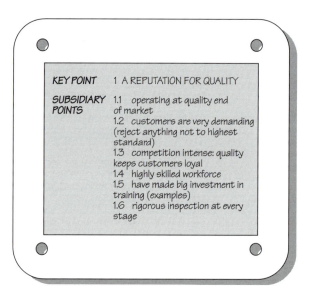

KEY POINT   1 A REPUTATION FOR QUALITY

SUBSIDIARY   1.1 operating at quality end
POINTS   of market
             1.2 customers are very demanding
             (reject anything not to highest
             standard)
             1.3 competition intense: quality
             keeps customers loyal
             1.4 highly skilled workforce
             1.5 have made big investment in
             training (examples)
             1.6 rigorous inspection at every
             stage

Start by drafting the main body of the speech: the introduction will practically write itself.

You now have a complete skeleton of the middle part of your speech, written out in logical order on separate sheets or cards. This simple outline can be the basis of the visual aids that you will produce.

4.3 The beginning and the end

Now you will need two more sheets or cards on which to draft out your introduction and conclusion.

Activity 41

Take one of the clean sheets or cards and head it INTRODUCTION.

Below that, write down, as briefly as you can, the various things you need to say in your introduction.

For example:

INTRODUCTION

- good afternoon etc.
- my name is . . .
- and I'm a team leader at . . .
- produce control systems
- up-to-date, high tech, forward-looking
- stop me if there's anything . . .
- happy to answer questions afterwards.

Activity 42

Now use another clean sheet to do the same thing for the SUMMARY AND CONCLUSION.

The conclusion needs a little thought. Think about what this particular group of listeners needs to know:

- your attitude to work experience students;
- what will be expected of them;
- what the students can expect to gain from the experience.

You should now have a set of up to ten sheets or cards, most of which should not have very much written on them.

Most of the hard work is now behind you. You have created a framework for the presentation. You now need to decide how exactly you are going to deliver it.

Remember – these are only your notes, not the speech itself.

Activity 43

2 mins

Some speakers prefer to write out their speech in full, and then read it word for word. This is perhaps because they feel there is less risk of making a mistake. Note down **one** disadvantage of doing this.

_____

_____

_____

If you just read out a full script:

■ it is likely to sound very artificial (it's difficult to write speech in a natural way);

■ your eyes will be focused on the paper most of the time (so you can't see the signals the people in the audience are sending you);

■ it will be difficult to establish 'rapport' – a two-way relationship – with the audience.

When you have rapport, you can keep the audience interested and 'carry them with you'. And equally, you can see what the audience is thinking, and how well you are getting through. If necessary you can adjust what you are saying.

Make eye contact with as many people in the audience as possible, looking from one to another in turn as you speak. Stay focused on each one for a few seconds.

5 Fleshing out your notes

Your notes give you a structure to work from. If you follow them, you will cover all the important points, in the right order, without missing any, and you will give your listeners what they want to hear.

But notes are just a series of lists. You need to turn them into speech, and to do this, you have to add words and phrases to link the various points together.

5.1 Turning notes into speech

Here's an example based on the introduction I suggested earlier. First, here is a reminder of the original notes, which are the bones of your presentation:

Here is an example of an introduction, based on Activity 41. I've left the original skeleton in capitals; the rest is the flesh which I would add to turn the notes into speech:

'GOOD AFTERNOON, and thank you for inviting me to come and speak to you. I hope you'll find it useful.'

[PAUSE]

'First let me introduce myself. MY NAME'S Sean Carter, and I work for Micron Products, which, as you probably know is about two miles from here on the Tegworth road. I'M A TEAM LEADER in the Clean Assembly Department. WE PRODUCE computerized CONTROL SYSTEMS – I'll explain that later – and my department does the most complicated part of the work. Micron is a very UP-TO-DATE firm, very HIGH-TECH, and very FORWARD-LOOKING when it comes to looking after our workforce.'

[PAUSE]

'I'm going to spend a few minutes telling you about our work. PLEASE STOP ME IF THERE'S ANYTHING you don't understand, because it can get a bit technical. Of course, I'll be HAPPY TO ANSWER QUESTIONS AFTERWARDS as well.'

Read this introduction out loud a couple of times. As you can tell:

- I used quite a lot of extra words to flesh out the basic notes;
- I used various links to try to make it fit together smoothly;
- I also took my time, and put in deliberate pauses where there were logical breaks in the flow.

Activity 44

15 mins

Now try turning your notes for an introduction to your presentation for teachers into a speech. Flesh it out so that it sounds sensible.

You will need to read it out loud. You could perhaps ask trusted friends or colleagues to listen and comment, or alternatively make an audio recording and play it back in private. Have several goes till you feel happy with it.

5.2 Using links

There are lots and lots of words and phrases you can use as links to help turn your notes into smoothly flowing speech:

- 'First I should explain that . . .'
- 'Secondly, . . .'
- 'Another important factor is that . . .'
- 'We also . . .'
- 'Naturally . . .'
- 'This means that . . .'
- 'You may also be surprised to learn that . . .'
- 'Of course, . . .'
- 'The next stage is . . .'
- 'On the other hand . . .'
- 'Finally, . . .'

The trick is to use as many different links as you can – with practice you will soon expand your collection. This will keep your speech sounding fresh and lively. Obviously, some links, like 'secondly' or 'finally', will only fit in certain places but there is no limit to the variations you can use. However:

- don't use the same link too often;
- don't put too much flesh on your notes – it may make your messages too hard for the listeners to spot.

5.3 Reaching a conclusion

How you begin and how you finish make quite an impression on your listeners. Of course the 'meat' of what you say is the most important part as far as you're concerned, but a good opening can get your listeners interested, alert, and on your side. A good finish can leave them with the impression of an interesting and well-organized contribution from you.

Activity 45

Look at the following examples and jot down whether you think each is good or bad and why you think that,

I   'Well, I – um – as you know, I haven't done much of this speaking so I – um – can't promise to do anything very much. But, as I've been called on to say a few words about work in my section – component assembly – well, here goes . . .'

2 'This is Jack's evening and we all know that Jack isn't one for speeches, He's already threatened me with what will happen if I make one, but we can't let him go, can we, without letting him know how much we . . .'

_____

_____

3 'For the last six months, we have been working (twenty-five hours a day sometimes) on the Delta project. As the section supervisor, I'd like to explain a bit about . . .'

_____

_____

4 'Well, I think that's about all . . . Yes, I think so. That's it then.'

_____

_____

5 'So the main thing for us is to keep up the same level of work in the next financial year. And for that we need your support. Thank you.'

_____

_____

Here are my comments.

Speaker 1

> Don't worry about the odd 'um' and 'er' – that's something everybody does.

Bad. Listening to this, you might sympathize with his nervousness but you wouldn't be impressed. If you say you're not going to be any good, listeners will tend to believe you. Don't apologize for yourself. By the time you stand up to speak, you are committed, so you might as well make the best of it.

This speaker is also rather slow to get going. We don't know anything about what he or she is going to talk about, only that the self-confidence to do it is lacking. It would be better to get to the point straight away as speaker 3 does.

Speaker 2

Good. This gets to the point in a friendly way and immediately gets listeners on the speaker's side ('but we can't let him go, can we . . .').

The performance is confident – the speaker makes a slight joke of the fact that Jack doesn't want speeches – and doesn't apologize for him- or herself.

65

Speaker 3

Good. This is really very similar to 2, although the situation is different. The speaker gets to the point straight away and makes a slight joke ('twenty-five hours a day sometimes') to establish a friendly relationship with the listeners.

Speaker 4

Bad. In the same way as you don't want to start to speak with an apology for yourself, so you don't want to finish by just letting your subject peter out. You can throw away a good, well-organized talk by such a feeble ending. This is why it is often useful to include in your notes exactly what you want the last line to be. Quite frequently, your listeners won't even know that you have missed out part of what you intended to say if you finish with a flourish.

Speaker 5

Good. This is much better than 4. The speaker repeats the main point of the speech very briefly ('the main thing for us is to keep up the same level of work …') and leaves listeners in no doubt about what is wanted from them.

And, having finished, the speaker stops – without any vague remarks about this being the end.

Notice, too, that the speaker thanks his or her listeners at this point. If you feel it is appropriate to thank your audience for their response, then this is the time to do it – at the end.

So we can now draw up a checklist of do's and don'ts to bear in mind when you are writing your speaking notes:

- don't apologize for yourself;
- do get to the point as soon as possible;
- don't use overworked language;
- do thank your audience at the end if it would be appropriate;
- don't just peter out – finish firmly.

6 Rehearsal and delivery

If you haven't done much public speaking before, the more practice you can get the better.

6.1 Practice and rehearsal

If you are tackling an important presentation for the first time, it would be worth planning a really thorough programme of practice and rehearsals, as follows.

Practice stage 1: private practice

Practise speaking from your notes somewhere private; try various different links and various amounts of flesh till you are happy with the way it sounds.

Practice stage 2: recording and playback

Talk through the whole presentation, still using your notes as the skeleton, and record it on audio cassette; play it back to see how it sounds; think about what might need changing.

Practice stage 3: private audition

Ask a colleague, friend or family member to be the audience, and deliver the presentation to them; ask them what they think, how natural it sounded, whether it was too fast, too slow, too complicated etc.

Practice stage 4: dress rehearsal

You should by this stage have ironed out any problems in your presentation; using your notes once more, rehearse it fully, complete with all your visual aids, to make sure that the whole performance fits together smoothly.

If you still have a little time before the day of the actual presentation, it would be worth while making another recording of the dress rehearsal and listening to it a few more times.

A lot of work?

Perhaps, but it will pay off on the day!

6.2 Speech day

Thorough preparation will give you extra confidence, but so far you haven't had to face a real audience – and that's when the pressure really goes on.

Activity 46

Think ahead to the day itself, and the moment when you have to stand up and start to speak in front of an expectant audience. In spite of all your preparation you will probably still feel nervous.

Be honest with yourself – deep down, what do you fear might go wrong?

Here are some of the things that speakers often worry about on the day, with my comments on them:

■ 'They're bound to know how nervous I am.'

No they won't – unless you show them or tell them. Keep control of your movements, and **never** give the game away by saying things like 'Please bear with me because I'm not very good at this', or 'Phew! I'm really glad that's over.'

■ 'I'm bound to fluff my words.'

No you aren't – provided you avoid long and difficult words, or words you aren't familiar with (Keep It Short and Simple!).

■ 'I'll lose my place and get flustered.'

No you won't – you've got your notes to guide you. If you lose your place in the notes, just pause for a few moments until you find it again; but **never** say 'Sorry, I've lost my place …' etc.

■ 'I'm sure I'll forget everything I want to say and dry up completely.'

No you won't – just carry on working steadily through your notes.

But if by any mischance something does go badly wrong:

■ don't show your audience you are rattled;
■ just pause and take your time to sort it out;
■ don't apologize;
■ don't ask for sympathy.

Show them you're in charge, and do what has to be done: that's what the audience expects.

6.3 Post-mortem and thinking about next time

No one does a perfect presentation first time round, because learning to speak effectively takes experience as well as preparation. To begin with, you should be more than satisfied if you cover the content thoroughly in the time available.

But when you have a few competent performances under your belt, it is time to think about polishing up your act.

Activity 47

Think back to the last few times you listened to someone giving a speech or a presentation. Think about how they delivered it, and especially their behaviour.

I'm sure they weren't perfect. But in what ways could they have improved their 'performance'?

_____

_____

_____

Some speakers are too technical, too quiet or too monotonous, but there is also a problem of annoying habits and mannerisms. These irritate the audience and distract them from the speech itself.

I don't know if you listed any of these little 'foibles' in Activity 47, but here are some that I have come across:

■ **irritating verbal mannerisms:**

- a speaker who kept using an irritating catch phrase: 'to be perfectly honest with you';
- a speaker who said 'y'know', 'er' and 'well' every few words: 'Well, er, it's, well, got a very good, y'know, reputation for, er, quality. Well . . .';
- a speaker who clears her throat nervously before each sentence;
- a speaker who always mutters under his breath when changing a visual aid: 'OK, right . . . OHP slide on . . . right . . . there we are . . . right';

■ **irritating physical mannerisms:**

- a speaker who always turns and talks to his flip-chart instead of facing the audience;
- a speaker who faces the audience, but never raises her eyes to look anyone in the face;
- a speaker who only looks at one person in the audience during the whole speech;
- a speaker who continually walks back and forth in front of the audience;
- a speaker who fiddles constantly, for instance by clicking his pen cap on and off;
- a speaker whose hands are always on the move: waving around, in and out of his pockets, picking something up from the table, putting it down again, scratching his head, back in his pockets, up again to rub his nose . . .;
- a speaker who is always hoisting his trousers up.

There are lots more bad habits like these – and they are almost all unconscious. Speakers simply don't realize they are doing these things.

69

Activity 48

20
mins

This Activity may provide the basis of appropriate evidence for your S/NVQ portfolio. If you are intending to take this course of action, it might be better to write your answers on separate sheets of paper.

Think very hard about your own verbal and physical mannerisms when speaking in public. Ask people who have watched you talking in some formal situation, or when the pressure is on you for some other reason.

If possible, arrange for someone to video you, and watch the tape together afterwards.

Now write down your mannerisms, as honestly as you can. Note which were most likely to distract or irritate the audience.

_____

_____

_____

_____

_____

Now practise speaking without these mannerisms. It's usually best to tackle them one at a time, making sure you've eliminated each one before going on to the next.

Of course, an occasional gesture to emphasize a point is fine, but anything beyond that will get in the way of your message, making you less professional than you could be.

Finally, here is a very straightforward task for you: sit down and watch the TV news.

- Watch the newsreaders carefully:

  - they are cool, calm, controlled and restrained;
  - they scarcely ever use a physical gesture, and they simply don't have any annoying mannerisms.

- Listen to them carefully:

  - the words they use are always simple and straightforward;
  - they speak clearly and without hurrying;
  - they've learned to use small changes in the tone and pitch of their voices to fit the 'story', whatever it is.

Watch and listen carefully, because these are the professionals. You and I may never reach those dizzy heights, but it is always worth remembering that once they were just like us. The only difference is that they have worked hard at it, practised their techniques and learned from long experience.

It's all a matter of learning the skills. They did it, and so can you.

Self-assessment 3

15 mins

1 What causes anxiety?

_____

_____

2 If you are anxious about something, you may try to avoid having to face it. What effect will this have in the longer term?

_____

3 The structure of a speech or presentation will always consist of three distinct parts. What are they, and what do they contain?

_____

_____

_____

4 Complete these sentences outlining three excellent reasons for using visual aids:

   a Some things are easier to _____ visually than in speech.

   b Visual aids help your listeners _____ the points you are making.

   c Visual aids make the whole presentation more _____ and _____.

5 Which way should you face when using:

   a a flip-chart; _____

   b an overhead or 35 mm projector. _____

6 What is the first thing you need to do in drafting an outline for a speech or presentation?

_____

7 What do we mean when we say a speaker has 'rapport'?

_____

8 This short extract from a speech contains **two** 'links'. Underline them:

'So that is why we need to upgrade customer contact skills. Before I leave that subject, let me stress the point again. Few customers notice good customer contact skills, but they all notice poor ones. Now, I want to go on to some practical matters . . .'

Answers to these questions can be found on page 87.

7 Summary

- Everyone is capable of becoming an effective speaker. It is a matter of learning the skills and techniques.

- Public speaking makes us nervous because it puts us under pressure and this causes the body to react as if there were a physical threat.

- We can deal with our anxious feelings by:

  - learning to control them;
  - becoming less sensitive to the threat;
  - recognizing that the threat itself is not serious;
  - improving our speaking technique, and thus our self-confidence;
  - careful planning.

- Planning for a formal presentation should cover six stages:

  - working out your objectives (why, who and where);
  - deciding the key points of the content;
  - working out a sensible structure;
  - selecting and preparing your visual aids;
  - making your outline notes;
  - practising and rehearsing.

- Using visual aids will make your speech or presentation more interesting and your messages more memorable.

- If you use visual aid equipment, make sure:

  - that you write or draw clearly and neatly;
  - that you don't try to cram in too much information;
  - that the equipment is working properly;
  - that you know how to use it;
  - that your visuals are clearly visible;
  - that you keep them short and simple;
  - that you talk to your audience, not the visuals.

- In any presentation, your introduction and conclusion are of major importance. Plan them carefully in advance.

- Your notes are the skeleton of your presentation, but you will need to:

  - use extra words to flesh them out;
  - use various links to make the ideas flow together smoothly;
  - take your time and remember to pause briefly when there is a logical break in the flow.

- If something goes wrong during the presentation:

  - don't show the audience you are rattled;
  - don't apologize;
  - don't ask for sympathy;
  - show them that you are in control.

Performance checks

Jot down your answers to the following questions on *Communicating in Groups.*

Question 1   Communication is often designed to achieve a practical objective. What does it always do?

_____

Question 2   The first half of the communication process is about sending clear and credible messages. What is the second half?

_____

Question 3   Why are visual means of communication so effective?

_____

Question 4   Messages are more credible when they come from an authoritative person. Apart from his or her formal title, what **four** things does authority depend on?

_____

_____

_____

_____

Question 5   What channel of communication can enable people in distant locations to see, hear and talk with each other?

_____

Question 6   How can a speaker make sure that body language reinforces his or her credibility?

_____

Question 7   What are 'standing orders' for a committee meeting?

_____

_____

73

Question 8 What 'formalities' – standard items – normally appear on the agenda for a meeting?

_____

_____

_____

_____

Question 9 When is the best time to make a contribution to a discussion?

_____

Question 10 Making good-quality contributions at a meeting helps the meeting work better. What **two** things does it do for the contributor?

_____

_____

Question 11 In a negotiation, what do we mean by the 'negotiable area'?

_____

Question 12 Janine was due to give a 15-minute talk to a group of trainee managers. How long should she spend preparing her talk?

_____

Question 13 **Three** things go to make an effective public speaker. What are they?

_____

_____

_____

Question 14 If something goes wrong during your presentation, what should you always try to show your audience?

_____

Question 15 What points would you expect to make in the introduction to a speech or presentation?

_____

_____

_____

_____

_____

Answers to these questions can be found on pages 89–90.

2 Workbook assessment

60 mins

Read the following case incidents and then deal with the questions that follow. Write your answers on a separate sheet of paper.

■ Kate was asked by her manager to arrange a meeting of representatives from seven different departments to discuss some problems that had occurred in processing customer orders. The objective was to draw up proposals for new revised procedures so as to prevent these problems recurring.

Kate had never organized a formal meeting like this before, and felt rather unsure of herself.

■ What administrative arrangements will Kate need to make for this meeting?

■ What difficulties is she likely to encounter?

■ Kate's manager was expecting to chair the meeting, but at the last moment, he was called to an unscheduled meeting with the directors. He told Kate to chair it herself. Kate had never chaired a formal meeting before, though she had been present at several. She did not feel very confident about this meeting, particularly since most of the people attending would be more senior than her.

■ What will Kate's main tasks be?
■ What difficulties is she likely to encounter?
■ What should happen if – as seems possible – the meeting is unable to finalize a list of recommendations within the time available?

3 Work-based assignment

60 mins

The time guide for this assignment gives you an approximate idea of how long it is likely to take you to write up your findings. You will find you need to spend some additional time gathering information, perhaps talking to colleagues and thinking about the assignment. The result of your efforts should be presented as speaking notes, draft visual aids, plus a recording on audio or video cassette.

Your written response to this assignment may form useful evidence for your S/NVQ portfolio. The assignment is designed to help you demonstrate your skills in:

- communicating;
- influencing others.

Prepare a presentation about **how the work of your team is organized, supervised and evaluated** – i.e. how you carry out your personal role as manager, supervisor or team leader. The audience is a visiting delegation from Germany. The members of the delegation all speak good, but not perfect English, and you will need to make allowances for this.

Follow the guidelines for planning and preparing a presentation given in Session C. It should not take more than 10 minutes in its final form.

- Make neat drafts of three flip-chart pages or three OHP slides, which you would propose to use as visual aids.
- Prepare a neat copy of the notes from which you would speak.
- Practise and rehearse delivering the presentation, perhaps with the help of friends.
- When you are happy with it, make an audio or video recording of the presentation (depending on what facilities you have available).

Remember that your presentation should cover all the key points, while not taking more than 10 minutes to deliver.

Reflect and review

1 Reflect and review

Now that you have completed your work on *Communicating in Groups,* let us review the objectives that we set at the beginning.

Our first objective was:

■ you will be better able to frame effective messages and choose the most appropriate channels through which to send them.

Really there are three broad issues here: how you formulate your messages, the channels you choose, and the style and manner in which you send them.

Your messages consist of information, instructions, requests, questions and so on. But they are competing with lots of other calls on people's attention. You must therefore do as much as you reasonably can to make sure that they reach their target and achieve the appropriate response.

The messages themselves must be clearly phrased, as brief as possible, and reasonably straightforward. It must be clear to the receiver what you are saying, what you want, when and how. This means thinking about your messages a bit, rather than simply launching into them.

■ Think about some of the messages – written or spoken – that you have sent in the last day or two. Could you have phrased any of them more effectively? How?

_____

_____

_____

To some extent, the way you frame your messages depends on the channels through which you choose to send them. More channels are available as digital technology develops, but the fundamental division is between situations where you can speak, and those where you have to write. Speech channels are in turn divided between face-to-face situations and the telephone. Where you can use body language and human contact, some advantages arise. However, there are also situations where writing is the better choice.

77

The ideal is to use the widest possible range of channels, choosing the best for each particular situation.

- If, like most people, you feel more comfortable with some channels than others, you ought to develop your ability to use your less favoured ones. What practical steps can you take to do this?

_____

_____

The next objective was

- you will be better able to plan and chair meetings.

Meetings are very important in organizations, but few people are ever given training in how to manage them. It tends to be a matter of learning by experience. Yet there is nothing specially difficult about planning and chairing meetings. It is simply a question of following well-understood procedures and guidelines.

Having said that, the more meetings you attend, the more comfortable you will be in that environment, and the better you will understand what works well and what does not. It is therefore a good idea to get that experience, and to think critically about the meetings that you attend.

- What can you do to get more experience of formal meetings and how they are organized and chaired?

_____

_____

People tend to think that everything about a meeting is the responsibility of the chairperson, but this is wrong. The participants share the responsibility, and they can make or break a meeting. Poor preparation, a negative attitude, laziness, self-indulgence and game-playing are all damaging. They are also self-defeating. Meetings take place for a reason, and they are part of the job for everyone who attends. Contributors who play a positive role can expect positive benefits.

Hence the next objective:

- you will be better able to prepare and make an effective contribution to a meeting.

An effective contribution is one which helps the work of the meeting, helps achieve the contributor's personal objectives, and enhances his or her reputation. The quality of your messages is important again here, as is the manner in which you deliver them. But preparation is also of great importance. You need to understand the issues, read the documents and have the facts at your fingertips. You may need to discuss the issues with your team, and lobby other people who will be attending the meeting.

In fact, you need to take the meeting seriously. And being well-prepared will also raise your confidence.

> ■ Use a separate piece of paper to make a checklist of what you will do to prepare for the next meeting you have to attend.

We also dealt with a subject that worries many managers, supervisors and team leaders considerably: giving a speech or presentation. Here our objective was:

■ you will be better able to plan, prepare and deliver an effective speech or presentation.

What is a 'good' speech or presentation? Simply one that keeps the listeners' attention and makes sure that the key points get through to them. Here, planning and preparation are at least half the battle. We spent some time explaining the stages of preparation in detail. The process began with an outline and continued by 'putting flesh on the bones'. The main emphasis was on getting the structure right, and on focusing on a small number of key points.

We also considered how to overcome anxiety, how to develop voice control, and the need to practise speaking from notes.

These are skills that come with practice. Take every reasonable opportunity to get that practice. Your practice 'speeches' don't have to be long – even a couple of minutes' worth can help – and you may find opportunities outside as well as inside work. It's also important to listen critically to other speakers, and note the techniques they use.

> ■ What steps will you take: a, to get practice in speaking publicly; and b, to watch and listen to more experienced speakers?

> _____

> _____

> _____

Careful planning, preparation and practice will improve your confidence, which will in turn improve your delivery. People aren't generally good listeners, so technique and skill are important. Our advice here is much the same as for any communication:

■ keep it short and simple;

■ **cut it down**: four or five key points are quite enough for a 15-minute session;

■ **slow it down**: your listeners are only human – they can only soak up your words so fast;

■ **focus**: deal with fire precautions only and leave fire-fighting and evacuation for another time;

79

- **organize**: present your points in a logical order so that they make sense;
- **check**: make sure each point has got through before you go on to the next; check again at the end;
- **repeat**: repeat each point and then sum them all up again at the end.

- What difference will all we have said make to the next speech or presentation that you give?

_____

_____

_____

2   Action plan

Use this plan to further develop for yourself a course of action you want to take. Make a note in the left-hand column of the issues or problems you want to tackle, and then decide what you intend to do, and make a note in Column 2.

The resources you need might include time, materials, information or money. You may need to negotiate for some of them, but they could be something easily acquired, like half an hour of somebody's time, or a chapter of a book. Put whatever you need in Column 3. No plan means anything without a timescale, so put a realistic target completion date in Column 4.

Finally, describe the outcome you want to achieve as a result of this plan, whether it is for your own benefit or advancement, or a more efficient way of doing things.

Desired outcomes	1 Issues	2 Action	3 Resources	4 Target completion	Actual outcomes

3 Extensions

Extension 1 Workbook   *Managing with Authority*
Author   Elaine Horrocks
Publisher   Pergamon Open Learning (NEBS Management Super Series 3)

Extension 2 Book   *Body Talk: the skills of positive image*
Author   Judi James
Edition   1995
Publisher   Industrial Society

Extension 3 Workbook   *Listening and Speaking*
Author   Howard Senter
Publisher   Pergamon Open Learning (NEBS Management Super Series 3)

Extension 4 *Breathing and voice control*

- Before you start to speak

  Take several slow, deep breaths. This will help calm you and get you ready to start.

- When you start speaking

  Take a deep breath and begin to speak as you are breathing out. Your breathing will be relaxed and the words are more likely to come out in an even flow in something like your normal voice.

  It can be a temptation to start to speak at the peak of a breath, especially if you're nervous, but this isn't a good idea. Your ribs are momentarily locked, so you haven't any real breath control, and breath and your words won't have much power behind them.

  Now the problem is how to produce enough sound to fill the room.

  Volume of sound comes not from your throat but from your chest. Once again, it's a question of getting the breathing right. If you breathe from as deep down in your chest as possible, you will find you are able to produce much more volume than your normal speaking voice, without the feeling of strain you have if you shout for more than a few seconds at a time.

  Trying to produce more volume from the **throat** won't work. It just puts a strain on your voice, and tends to produce a rather reedy, thin speaking voice which isn't very enjoyable to listen to.

  This is one of the reasons why people's voices tend to rise when they are nervous. The other reason is a nervous tightening of the throat muscles which restricts the air flow.

82

Although breath control makes a lot of difference to how successfully you can make yourself heard, there are a few simple techniques which will improve your performance further.

■ Keep your chin tilted up slightly.

Not so far that you get a crick in your neck or you can't see your notes. But if you make a conscious effort to keep your head up slightly, it stops you directing your voice down towards the floor, and helps your voice to carry to the back of the room.

■ Talk slightly nasally.

If you haven't got a very powerful voice you can make it carry better if you talk slightly more through your nose than usual. It helps if you think in terms of talking with a slight American accent – but make it slight,

■ Direct your voice round the room.

Move your head slightly. Speak towards all your listeners in turn wherever they are sitting. Concentrate especially on those sitting near the back.

Extension 5

Audio cassette set	*Relaxation for Anxiety*
Authors	George Ward (text), Mike Burridge (music)
Publisher	The Anxiety Disorders Association, 20 Church Street, Dagenham, Essex. RM10 9UR. Tel. 0181 491 4700. First published 1995.

Extension 6   *Using visual aids*

The **overhead projector** (OHP) is one of the simplest and most effective visual aids. It is particularly valuable for keeping important points in front of your listeners while you are talking about them. OHPs are useful for diagrams, cartoons and other illustrations, as well as text.

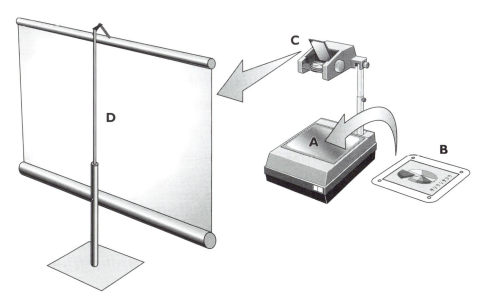

It is basically a box with a back-lit opaque panel on the top (A). You place your slide (B) on top of this panel, and the lens (C) picks up the image and casts it onto a screen (D). This creates a greatly enlarged image, big enough for the audience to read.

Making OHP slides is very easy. The slides themselves are made of heat-resistant plastic film, and all you need to write on them is one or two special felt-tip pens in different colours. The techniques for successful OHP slides are:

OHP slides can also be prepared on a computer and printed out through a laser or ink-jet printer. You can add colour by hand if necessary.

■ write or draw clearly;
■ write or draw neatly;
■ don't try to cram on too much information.

In fact it is most important to draft out your OHP sheet on plain paper, to make sure you have got it right before you put pen to plastic!

Here are two examples of OHP slides, both much reduced from the normal size of about 20 cm × 30 cm:

Bad

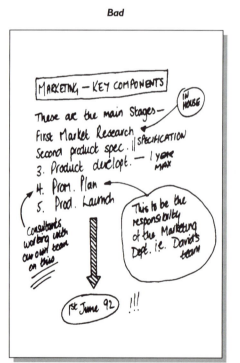

Good

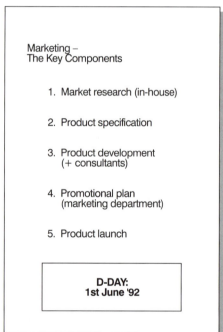

When you are talking about what the slide shows, you can point to particular parts of it, and there are techniques for this too:

■ use a pencil or a pointer and point to the slide itself, not the screen (the lens will project the pointer onto the screen);
■ keep facing the audience, and don't be tempted to turn round and look at the screen while you are talking (this is bad body language and also makes you hard to hear).

Other commonly used visual aids include:

- **35mm slide projectors** – professional but may be expensive

  Slides can be produced quickly using special computer software and/or with the help of a photographer;

- **video**, via TV screen or video projector – increasingly acceptable for showing locations, processes and short interviews

  Hand-held cameras are widely available and easy to use, but there is a temptation to make video sequences too long

- **computer-based presentations** – effective but only suitable for a small intimate audience and require expertise to create

  Several software packages, mainly designed for sales presentations and internal meetings, are available, and can reach a wider audience via a computer network.

  Extensions 1, 2, 3 and 5 can be taken up via your NEBS Management Centre. They will either have them or will arrange that you have access to them. However, it may be more convenient to check out the materials with your personnel or training people at work – they may well give you access. There are other good reasons for approaching your own people; for example, they will become aware of your interest and you can involve them in your development.

4 Answers to self-assessment questions

Self-assessment 1 on page 20

1 The hidden agenda in all communication is the effect it has on **FEELINGS AND ATTITUDES** and **WORKING RELATIONSHIPS**.

2 Statement a is aggressive; statement b is unassertive; statement c is assertive – definite and clear but still polite and without any aggressiveness.

3 The well-known sayings are:

I **HEAR** and I forget.
I **SEE** and I **REMEMBER**.
I do and I **UNDERSTAND**.

4 The four things that help give someone real, as opposed to formal authority, are:

EXPERTISE
COMPETENCE
FAIRNESS
CONSISTENCY

85

5   Digital electronic channels of communication include fax and e-mail, but telephone conversations are also digital, and the same applies to video links.

6   Members of teams:

a know **EACH OTHER**:
b share **VALUES AND GOALS**;
c possess **A SENSE OF COMMON IDENTITY AND TEAM SPIRIT**;

while members of random groups do not.

7   If you know the nature of any objections to the case you are intending to put forward, you will avoid being 'ambushed' and can deal with them in your own contribution.

8   A speaker's body language can:

a reduce the speaker's credibility when it is distracting;
b weaken the message when it conflicts with it.

Self-assessment 2 on page 47

1   A committee is 'a body of persons appointed or elected for some special business or purpose.'

2   The two main purposes of regular formal meetings are:

a for better communication;
b for better management control.

3   A control cycle is the process of monitoring information about activities and deciding to take action to modify them.

4   Participants in a meeting should prepare themselves beforehand by:

a reading the documents;
b seeking clarification if necessary;
c making notes about what they want to contribute.

5   The chairperson of a meeting must resist the temptation to speak too much.

6   Seating arrangements at a meeting have significance because they can imply (or reinforce) unequal status among those present. This can inhibit younger and more junior people from making their rightful contribution.

7   a There should certainly be some flexibility, but it is a bad idea to let people add items freely. The meetings will go on too long, and people won't be able to prepare properly for the discussions.
    b This is a very bad idea – such a verbatim transcript could run to dozens of pages and would be expensive to produce and daunting to read.
    c It certainly is a problem – people are often asked to participate in a meeting precisely because their contribution is wanted. But talking too much is perhaps in practice more of a problem.

8 If one side clearly loses in a negotiation, the risks are that:

a someone more senior on the losing side may repudiate the agreement;
b the losing negotiator may feel resentful and seek vengeance at a later date.

Self-assessment 3 on page 71

1 Anxiety is the body's automatic reaction to a situation in which it believes – sometimes wrongly – that it is facing a serious threat.

2 If you manage to avoid something – making a public speech, for example – about which you feel anxious, you will feel relieved in the short-term, but:

■ you may only have postponed the 'crunch';
■ it is a scientific fact that avoiding the thing you are anxious about only makes the anxiety worse in the longer term.

3 A speech or presentation will always consist of:

a a beginning (the introduction);
b a middle (the main part of the presentation);
c an end (the summary and conclusions).

4 These sentences should read:

a Some things are easier to **COMMUNICATE** visually than in speech.
b Visual aids help your listeners **REMEMBER** the points you are making.
c Visual aids make the whole presentation more **INTERESTING** and **CREDIBLE**.

5 Whatever kind of visual aids you are using, **YOU SHOULD ALWAYS FACE THE AUDIENCE.**

6 The first thing you need to do in drafting an outline for a speech or presentation is to **LIST THE KEY POINTS THAT YOU WANT TO MAKE.**

7 Rapport is a good two-way relationship between the speaker and the audience.

8 I have underlined the two sections that I consider to be links:

'So that is why we need to upgrade customer contact skills. <u>Before I leave that subject</u>, let me stress the point again. Few customers notice good customer contact skills, but they all notice poor ones. <u>Now, I want to go on to</u> some practical matters . . .'

5 Answers to activities

**Activity 6
on page 9**

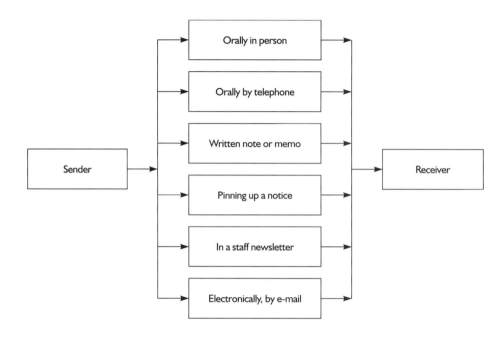

**Activity 13
on page 18**

Common signals that you might have listed are:

- shaking the head to show disagreement;
- beckoning;
- waving to attract attention;
- waving both hands from side to side to indicate 'stop';
- pointing;
- clapping;
- shrugging the shoulders to indicate 'don't know' or 'don't care';
- raising the arms to surrender;
- shaking a fist to show anger.

**Activity 17
on page 27**

You may have used slightly different words to describe the control process, but basically the cycle should be something like this:

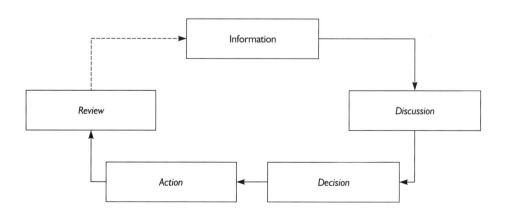

6 Answers to the quick quiz

Answer 1   Communication always affects the relationships between the people involved – even if only in a very small way.

Answer 2   The second half of the communication process is getting feedback to confirm that the message has got through.

Answer 3   Visual means of communication are effective because humans are better at understanding and remembering visual information than verbal information.

Answer 4   Authority depends on the person being able to demonstrate:

■ expertise;
■ competence;
■ fairness;
■ consistency in making decisions.

Answer 5   The only channel of communication that can enable people in distant locations to see, hear and talk with each other is a videoconferencing link.

Answer 6   Body language reinforces credibility when it's consistent with the messages the person is communicating.

Answer 7   Standing orders are the rules for running a particular type of meeting.

Answer 8   The standard formalities that usually appear on a meeting agenda are:

■ Apologies for absence;
■ Minutes of the last meeting;
■ Matters arising;
■ Any other business;
■ Date of next meeting.

Answer 9   The best time to make a contribution to a discussion at a meeting is near the beginning. People who wait till the end, or speak too frequently, tend to lose credibility.

Answer 10   Good-quality contributions help the contributor achieve the outcomes he or she is seeking; they also improve his or her personal standing and career prospects.

Answer 11   In a negotiation, the 'negotiable area' is the area where the two sides' maximum and minimum positions overlap, and where agreement will eventually be reached.

Answer 12   Janine should spend **at least 75 minutes** preparing her talk. Most speakers find they need at least five times as long to prepare a talk than to deliver it.

Answer 13   The three things that go to make an effective public speaker are:

- determination;
- practice;
- learning the necessary skills.

Answer 14   If something goes wrong during your presentation, you should you always try to show your audience that you are still in control.

Answer 15   In the introduction to a speech or presentation you might expect:

- to greet the audience;
- to introduce yourself;
- to explain what you are going to talk about;
- to explain the procedure (how long, what about questions etc.);
- in some cases, to give a brief summary of the main topics.

7 Certificate

Completion of this certificate by an authorized person shows that you have worked through all the parts of this workbook and satisfactorily completed the assessments. The certificate provides a record of what you have done that may be used for exemptions or as evidence of prior learning against other nationally certificated qualifications.

Pergamon Open Learning and NEBS Management are always keen to refine and improve their products. One of the key sources of information to help this process are people who have just used the product. If you have any information or views, good or bad, please pass these on.

NEBS MANAGEMENT DEVELOPMENT

SUPER SERIES

THIRD EDITION

Communicating in Groups

....

has satisfactorily completed this workbook

Name of signatory ....

Position ....

Signature ....

Date ....

Official stamp

SUPER SERIES

To Order - phone us direct for prices and availability details (please quote ISBNs when ordering)
College orders: 01865 314333 • Account holders: 01865 314301
Individual purchases: 01865 314627 (please have credit card details ready)

We Need Your Views

We really need your views in order to make the Super Series 3 (SS3) an even better learning tool for you. Please take time out to complete and return this questionnaire to Sarah Scott-Taylor, Pergamon Open Learning, Linacre House, Jordan Hill, Oxford, OX2 8DP.

Name: ....

Address: ....

....

Title of workbook: ....

If applicable, please state which qualification you are studying for. If not, please describe what study you are undertaking, and with which organisation or college:

....

Please grade the following out of 10 (10 being extremely good, 0 being extremely poor):

Content   ....   Appropriateness to your position   ....

Readability   ....   Qualification coverage   ....

What did you particularly like about this workbook?

....
....
....

Are there any features you disliked about this workbook? Please identify them.

....
....
....

Are there any errors we have missed? If so, please state page number: ....

How are you using the material? For example, as an open learning course, as a reference resource, as a training resource etc.

....

How did you hear about Super Series 3?:

Word of mouth: ☐   Through my tutor/trainer: ☐   Mailshot: ☐

Other (please give details): ....

....

Many thanks for your help in returning this form.